# PORNOGRAPHY

*Also by*
*Carol Gorman*
*America's Farm Crisis*

# PORNOGRAPHY

CAROL
GORMAN

*Franklin Watts*
*New York/London*
*Toronto/Sydney*
*1988*

Library of Congress Cataloging in Publication Data

Gorman, Carol.
Pornography / by Carol Gorman.
p. cm.
Bibliography: p.
Includes Index.
Summary: Discusses aspects of the issue of pornography, including
problems that arise when trying to define what material is dangerous
to society, what should be outlawed, and should the individual have
the right to decide for himself.
ISBN 0-531-10591-1
1. Pornography—Social aspects—United States—Juvenile
literature. [1. Pornography.] I. Title.
HQ144.G73    1988
363.4'7—dc19

*To my husband Ed*
*for his unwavering support*

# CONTENTS

# PORNOGRAPHY

# A WORD FROM
# THE AUTHOR

The following book deals with one of the most controversial topics of our time, pornography. Much has been written and said on both sides of the issue, not all of it accurate or "true" in an objective, scientific sense.

So here and now, the author would like to alert readers that a great deal of what follows—in the quotes from people and periodicals—falls into the category of opinion rather than fact.

Pornography is a moral and political issue, not a scientific one. For this reason, the author makes no comments on the opinions expressed herein, but in the interest of fairness, lets those opinions be stated. It is for the reader to be the judge of the statement's validity or lack thereof.

Carol Gorman

# INTRODUCTION

Anne, a high school student, is moving with her family into a house across town that used to be owned by a friend of her father's.

Her new room had been occupied by a sixteen-year-old boy named Tom whom she had met once at a party. This room is bigger than the one in Anne's old house, and she's anxious to move in her things and make it her own.

Anne opens the closet door and climbs on a stepstool to reach the top shelf. A box at the back catches her eye, and she pulls it forward, curious.

She slides the top off of the box and sees that it is filled with magazines. The top two are for fishing and boating enthusiasts. But when she lifts these up, she finds a stack of pornographic magazines. These magazines feature pictures of nude or nearly nude women and men in various sexual poses. But the magazines that really surprise and shock Anne are those that picture women as victims in dangerous or violent situations. These photographs strongly suggest brutality and rape.

Anne wonders why Tom would be interested in this type of magazine. Does his reading of these magazines indicate that he has angry or malevolent feelings about women? He had been very polite when she had met him, and seemed to have a good sense of humor.

Is Tom going through a phase? Anne wonders if *all* men look at pornography. Does her father? Her older brother? And why? Are they curious? Anne notices that in many of the pictures, even the nonviolent ones, the men are in dominant poses, suggesting that they have power over the women. But the women have expressions indicating that they are enjoying their subservient roles. Do most couples view sex in this way?

Anne feels uncomfortable about the way sex is portrayed in these magazines. She wonders if she is being prudish, and if other people, particularly men, feel the same way.

Anne has heard stories on the news about religious organizations picketing convenience stores, trying to force store owners to stop carrying pornographic magazines. She and her mother saw a picket line in front of a local video store that carried pornographic films as well as Oscar winners and family favorites.

Anne has also read magazine articles in which legal experts were quoted as saying that any American has the right to look at or read anything he or she desires under the rights provided for by the First Amendment to the Constitution.

Who is right? Anne wonders. She does not like pornography, but she does not know where she should stand on the issue for others. Does pornography change the behavior of its readers? Does it hurt anyone?

These questions are asked frequently by different groups of people, with equal fervor. Each group brings its own set of values and interests to the issue of pornography.

In this book, we will examine pornography from several different viewpoints. We will look at what religious and legal experts have to say, and we will hear from feminists and business people about their concerns.

Pornography is a difficult and emotional topic, involving many complex issues. We will examine these issues and let readers decide for themselves where they stand on the controversial topic of pornography.

# PORNOGRAPHY: SHOULD IT BE LEGAL?

The First Amendment to the United States Constitution provides for (in addition to freedom of religion) freedom of the press and freedom of speech for all Americans. This amendment, the first of ten known as the Bill of Rights, was written to insure that the government would not interfere with individual rights.

There are limits to these freedoms, however. The First Amendment does not protect certain types of speech and writing that could be harmful to the government or individuals.

For instance, suppose an author writes a story in a magazine that contains lies about someone. The law provides that the person who is injured because of the lies can sue the writer and publisher of the magazine for *libel*.

Speech that can be dangerous to life, property, or national security is not protected by the First Amendment. Examples are words that incite to violence or treasonous language used while spying against the United States.

But sometimes, as in the case of pornography, there are problems that arise when we try to define which words are dangerous and which words are harmless. Some people think that pornography should be outlawed as dangerous to society. Others believe that individuals should have the right to decide whether or not pornography is right for them.

Who is right? Should pornography be legal? Let's examine what the courts have said about this issue.

One of the biggest problems the courts have addressed is how to define pornography.

"Pornography" has always had a derogatory connotation. It comes from the Greek word "*pornographos*," which interpreted means to describe prostitutes and their trade.

There can be confusion in a discussion of pornography because often the word "pornography" is used as a general word to cover everything from soft-core "erotica" (writing which seeks to arouse sexually in a nongraphic manner) to sexually graphic, "hard-core" porn. People sometimes react differently to "pornography," depending upon the degree of explicitness a particular piece of material uses.

Because so many Americans use the word "pornography" in discussions of sexual material, however, we will use that word generally throughout this book. When it is necessary to distinguish the type of pornography to which we are referring, we will be specific.

The law uses the word "obscenity" when dealing with questions of legality, and the courts are the final decision-makers on what is or is not obscene.

At the beginning of the twentieth century, the United States was using the definition for obscenity supplied by

Lord Cockburn in the case *Regina* v. *Hicklin*, which had been brought before the English courts in 1868.[1]

In that case, Lord Cockburn declared material was obscene that tended to "deprave and corrupt" the minds of those readers who were open to immoral influences.

This definition was challenged in American courts in the early 1900s. In *United States* v. *Kennerly* (1913), Judge Learned Hand severely criticized Lord Cockburn's test for two reasons. First, he said, the *Hicklin* definition judged written material by whether those most susceptible would be corrupted. Since children are likely to be the most susceptible, he said this test "would reduce our treatment of sex to the standards of a child's library in the supposed interest of a salacious few. . . ." Judge Hand also disapproved of the *Hicklin* definition because it allowed a whole work to be judged on the basis of specific passages taken out of context, instead of judging the work as a whole.

In spite of his criticism of the *Hicklin* decision, Hand used the definition it supplied because he said he was required to follow the precedent established to determine whether or not material was obscene.[2]

The Hicklin case was challenged again in 1933 in *United States* v. *One Book Entitled Ulysses*. The court ruled that the book *Ulysses*, by James Joyce, was not obscene, and it set forth a new test for obscenity.

This stated that a work was obscene if, first, it was written with "pornographic intent," and if so, if it tended to "stir the lustful thoughts" of a reader. If the author did not have pornographic intent, then a court would have to judge it by its effect on an average member of the community. The court also ruled in the *Ulysses* case that a work in question must be judged in its entirety, or as a whole, rather than in isolated, fragmented pieces.

Even though this case weakened the influence of the *Hicklin* definition, many state and federal courts still used the 1868 definition supplied by *Hicklin*.[3]

As late as the 1950s, there was little uniformity in the courts about how to define obscenity.

Up to this point, the United States Supreme Court had ruled on several cases about obscenity, but it had not addressed the issue of whether obscenity was lawful under the First Amendment to the Constitution.

In 1957, in the case *Roth* v. *United States*, the Supreme Court ruled that obscene material was not protected under the Constitution, and that the First Amendment had never been intended to cover "every utterance." Justice William Brennan, writing on behalf of the majority, said that the First Amendment had originally been written to allow "unfettered interchange of ideas for the bringing about of political and social changes desired by the people," and that obscene material supplied little, if any, social value.

The Supreme Court went on to define obscene material as that which "deals with sex in a manner appealing to the prurient interest." "Prurient," according to the court, and quoted in Daniel S. Moretti, author of *Obscenity and Pornography: The Law under the First Amendment*, meant "material having a tendency to excite lustful thoughts."

The Court set forth two tests to determine if material was obscene. In the first, a work would have to be judged obscene if to the "average person applying contemporary community standards, the dominant theme of the material taken as a whole appeals to the prurient interest." In the

*Police burn seized obscene literature in New York City in 1935. The man in the center is the secretary to the New York Society for the Suppression of Vice.*

second test, the court said that material should be examined to determine whether the work is "utterly without redeeming social importance." If a work provided ideas of social importance, even though it appealed to the prurient interest, it could not be ruled obscene.[4]

Several cases brought before the Supreme Court modified the *Roth* standard of what was obscene, bringing that standard closer to a definition of what is considered "hard-core" pornography.

But the biggest problem with the *Roth* definition remained: what would be considered "redeeming social importance"? As Moretti points out in his book, *Obscenity and Pornography*, it began to look as if the Supreme Court would have to decide whether each individual example of questionable material was obscene.

In 1965, the Supreme Court supplied a three-part test of obscenity in the case *Memoirs* v. *Massachusetts*. (*Memoirs of a Woman of Pleasure* by John Cleland.) First, the material must be "patently offensive." Second, the overall theme of the material must appeal to the "prurient interest." And third, the material must have no redeeming social value. This definition in effect narrowed the legal definition of obscenity to that which might be considered "hard-core."

After the 1965 *Memoirs* decision, it became even more difficult legally to label anything "obscene," since "prurient interest" was hard to define and most material contained at least some "social importance."[5]

In 1973, the Supreme Court, with its then-new Chief Justice, Warren Burger, handed down an important decision that remains the foundation by which a work is ruled obscene. The case was *Miller* v. *California*. Miller had been convicted of mass-mailing brochures that advertised sex-oriented books. In a five-to-four decision, the Supreme Court upheld Miller's conviction. It tightened the earlier *Roth* decision that obscenity was not protected by

First Amendment rights and set forth a new test for deciding whether or not material was obscene.

This new test was similar to the test previously used in *Roth*, but it had several important differences. The biggest difference was that a work did not have to be "utterly without redeeming social value" in order to be considered obscene. Instead, Chief Justice Burger held that a work not having "serious literary, artistic, political or scientific value" could be judged obscene. This small change from the *Roth* definition made it easier to find a work obscene. Another difference was that the Court went a step further and gave examples of what it considered "patently offensive": "(a) Patently offensive representations or descriptions of ultimate sexual acts, normal or perverted, actual or simulated. (b) Patently offensive representations or descriptions of masturbation, excretory functions, and lewd exhibition of the genitals."

The *Miller* decision went on to state: "Under the holdings announced today, no one will be subject to prosecution for the sale or exposure of obscene materials unless these materials depict or describe patently offensive 'hardcore' sexual conduct specifically defined by the regulating state law, as written or construed."

The ruling also required that a work be judged by the prevailing attitudes and values of the community in which the obscenity trial takes place, and not by a national standard. Chief Justice Burger pointed out that people in Maine or Mississippi might have differing views on conduct than those living in Las Vegas or New York City.[6]

As we have seen, the Supreme Court has ruled that obscenity is not protected under the First Amendment. So the question of whether or not pornography is legal is determined in the courts by evaluating each case individually and by applying "community standards" in order to determine whether or not each is obscene.

There are several groups of people who have used the

The 1973 Supreme Court ruling on obscenity set forth that, among other things, "community standards" be applied in determining whether something is obscene. This adult bookstore in Cincinnati, Ohio was closed following the court decision.

print and electronic media to talk about pornography and voice their opinions on the subject. In the following chapters, we will examine some of these groups and hear what they have to say about pornography, First Amendment rights, and public morals.

# PORNOGRAPHY
# AND CENSORSHIP

Although many Americans oppose pornography, there is little agreement about what, if anything, should be done about it. The major argument against censoring porn is that censorship of any kind has no place in a free country that guarantees free speech and a free press.

The controversy over pornography has split many feminist groups across the country. Some of these women claim there is a link between the use of pornography and violence against women, and that pornography degrades women by promoting them as "sexual objects" for men. Others are concerned that censorship may, at some point, be used to silence their own voices.

Lois P. Sheinfeld, an attorney and Associate Professor of Journalism and Mass Communications at New York

University, is concerned that the civil rights argument is clouding the important issue of First Amendment rights. In the September 8, 1984, issue of *The Nation*, she wrote:

*Repudiation of the free speech principles of the First Amendment marks the current antipornography campaign as the new censorship. Under the banner of civil rights, its proponents seek to suppress free expression by state proscription of books, magazines, films, plays and the visual arts. . . .*

*Unless it can be factually demonstrated that speech causes severe harm, the First Amendment denies to any official the power to decide what people may or may not see and hear. The public, not the government, determines the acceptability and value of ideas. "Fear of serious injury cannot alone justify suppression of free speech. . . . Men feared witches and burnt women," warned Justice Louis Brandeis. . . .*

*Censorship is not advocated by everyone who opposes pornography, and antipornography censorship is not supported by all feminists. As a feminist, I am troubled by a campaign that exalts bookburning in the name of women's rights. Official repression of disfavored expression places all expression, and essential liberty, in jeopardy. Without fidelity to the constitutional commands that assure open and free discourse, the struggle for sexual equality itself is at risk.*

Two women who have received media attention are antipornography activists Andrea Dworkin, a writer, and Catharine MacKinnon, a law professor at the University of Minnesota. They wrote a controversial antipornography civil ordinance for the city of Minneapolis.

In a paper presented to the Minneapolis City Council on December 26, 1983, they wrote:

—27

*Most frequently, pornography promotes rape, pain, humiliation and inferiority as experiences that are sexually pleasing to all women because we are women. The studies show that it is not atypical for men to believe and act on the pornography. Each time men are sexually aroused by pornography— the sexually explicit subordination of women—they learn to connect women's sexual pleasure to abuse and women's sexual nature to inferiority.*[1]

A *Newsweek* article of March 18, 1985, quotes Dworkin as saying: "Pornography creates attitudes that keep women second-class citizens. Porn teaches men that what they see reflects our natural attitudes."

The city ordinance that Dworkin and MacKinnon wrote allowed anyone who had been forced to participate in, or look at pornography, or anyone who had been attacked or injured in any way directly caused by a particular piece of pornographic material, to make a formal complaint with the Human Rights Commission or to go to court. It also provided for individuals to take the pornography sellers to court. The Human Rights Commission or the court would then determine whether or not that piece of material was pornographic as defined by the ordinance.

This is the definition of pornography outlined in the ordinance:

*Pornography is a form of discrimination on the basis of sex. Pornography is the sexually explicit subordination of women, graphically depicted, whether in pictures or in words, that also includes one or more of the following:*

*1. women are presented as sexual objects, things, or commodities; or*

*2. women are presented as sexual objects who enjoy pain or humiliation; or*

3. *women are presented as sexual objects who experience sexual pleasure in being raped; or*

4. *women are presented as sexual objects tied up or cut up or mutilated or bruised or physically hurt; or*

5. *women are presented in postures of sexual submission; or*

6. *women's body parts—including but not limited to vaginas, breasts, and buttocks—are exhibited, such that women are reduced to those parts or such that the subordinate sexual status of women is reinforced; or*

7. *women are presented as whores by nature; or*

8. *women are presented being penetrated by objects or animals; or*

9. *women are presented in scenarios of degradation, injury, abasement, torture, shown as filthy or inferior, bleeding, bruised, or hurt in a context that makes these conditions sexual.*[2]

MacKinnon and Dworkin say they are protecting civil rights: women's right to be free from harm. In the March 18, 1985 *Newsweek* article, MacKinnon says, "When you see what the effects of pornography are, any woman is a target. Given that we know that some number of men are looking at some amount of pornography, we can tell you that the . . . abuse will happen. All that we can't tell is to which individual it will happen."

This Minneapolis ordinance was vetoed by the mayor. It passed the city council a second time, but was again defeated by mayoral veto.

Donald M. Fraser, the mayor of Minneapolis, explained his reasons for vetoing the proposed ordinance in a letter to the Minneapolis City Council:

*The remedy sought through the ordinance as drafted is neither appropriate nor enforceable within our cherished tradition and constitutionally protected right of free speech. The definition of pornography in the ordinance is so broad and so vague as to make it impossible for a bookseller, movie theater operator or museum director to adjust his or her conduct in order to keep from running afoul of its proscriptions. The ordinance needs more analysis and redrafting before a final judgment can be made as to whether or not it would then represent sound public policy and should be adopted.*[3]

Fraser goes on to explain how the ordinance was to work. A panel from the Civil Rights Commission would, in essence, determine what could be sold, distributed, or displayed in the city. "When issues of free speech are raised, granting the decision-making power to an administrative panel is troubling to me. Some might call it a Board of Censors."

Fraser points out in his letter that obscene material is already illegal by law. He contends that the drafted ordinance seeks to ban sexually explicit material that is degrading to women even though it is not obscene and therefore protected under the First Amendment.

Fraser noted MacKinnon and Dworkin's charge that obscene material impairs other rights of women and stated that more research and analysis is needed to determine the validity of that constitutional question.

Fraser's final objection was that the ordinance does not provide for the defense that the defendant did not

*Television star Valerie Harper and other women demonstrate against pornography in New York.*

know or intend the material to be pornographic or discriminatory against women. "The chilling effect of an overly broad ordinance is well known," he wrote.[4]

Similar ordinances were proposed in such cities as Indianapolis (passed but struck down in court) and Los Angeles. Whether or not they passed, these moves represented a victory for MacKinnon and Dworkin, said Burt Neuborne, legal director of the American Civil Liberties Union, who was against the proposed ordinances. In the March 18, 1985 *Newsweek* article, Neuborne said of MacKinnon, "[She's] changed the way people think about a problem. She's telling people that porn is not cute, it has social ramifications, it's a symbol of a serious social malaise in the country. What racist speech was to racism, pornography is to sex discrimination."

Many feminists strongly disagreed with MacKinnon and Dworkin's proposed ordinance. Marcia Pally, a writer and critic, wrote in *The Nation* on June 29, 1985:

> *The Feminist Anti Censorship Taskforce (FACT), with independent offices in New York, Los Angeles, San Francisco, Toronto, and Madison, Wisconsin, is concerned not only about the legislation's potential damage to First Amendment rights but about its possible misuse. Conservatives, for example, might employ the law to remove from the bookstore shelves sexually explicit gay or feminist materials—the health manual* Our Bodies, Ourselves, *for example—because they find such materials degrading to women. . . .*
>
> *Will removing* Playboy *from the A&P stop rape, discrimination or the feminization of poverty? Since battery, incest and inequality flourished for thousands of years before the mass-market porn industry, it's unlikely that they're directly linked to "dirty pictures." It's unlikely, too, that porn initiates violence or lousy pay.*

Sol Gordon, a professor of child and family studies at Syracuse University, says, "Pornography is not a cause of anything. It is a symptom. . . . The wildest imagination leads us to believe that you can ban pornography. . . . I think those laws are an outrageous violation of civil liberties. You could use them to ban Erica Jong; you could ban the Bible. The Bible is one of the most masochistic, pornographic things we have in terms of humiliation of women."[5]

In a panel discussion of pornography reported in *Harper's* in November 1984, Erica Jong, a novelist and poet, says,

> *To understand the function of pornography we have to distinguish it from erotica. Erotica celebrates the erotic nature of the human creature, attempts to probe what is erotic in the human soul and the human mind, and does so artfully, dramatically. Pornography, on the other hand, serves simply as an aid to masturbation, with no artistic pretensions and no artistic value. . . . Today's pornography . . . shows us in sharp relief the sickness of our society, the twisted attitudes toward sex that persist beneath the facade of gentility. . . .*
>
> *But we cannot legislate these attitudes out of existence. . . . I believe that censorship only springs back against the givers of culture—against authors, artists, and feminists, against anybody who wants to change society. . . . The history of censorship is full of hideous examples of great works of art— books like* Ulysses, The Return of the Native, *and* Tropic of Cancer—*being censored while trash has gone free.*

Also on the panel was Midge Decter, executive director of the Committee for the Free World. She said, "Can we not at the very least distinguish between books and shows that we read and view voluntarily and the pornography displayed at the newsstands and on movie marquees, which we are forced to see?"

Susan Brownmiller, a founder of Women Against Pornography, answered, "Yes, we can certainly impose restrictions on public displays of pornography without violating the First Amendment. I want to protect free speech. I would never say, 'Smash the presses! Don't let Al Goldstein [publisher of *Screw* magazine] put out his smut sheet!' I think he has a right to publish it. But I don't think he can claim he has the right to display his magazine on the newsstands because it is protected speech."

Aryeh Neier, a former national executive director of the American Civil Liberties Union, said: "The legal term generally used when we talk about restricting public displays is 'thrusting,' that is, large public displays that someone cannot avoid seeing. I agree that we can regulate such displays without interfering with anyone's right to read what he wants, see what he wants, and express himself as he wants. . . . When the person who disseminates imposes his images on an unwilling audience, he may be interfering with the freedom of choice of that audience."

Al Goldstein replied, "I would agree to [a restriction of public displays of *Screw*], Susan—but only if you agreed to restrict *Ms.* as well. . . .

"In a democracy, a lot of things offend *someone*. . . . Totalitarian countries eliminate this problem; people don't have to worry about choosing between various points of view because there is no choice."

Beverly P. Lynch, university librarian at the University of Illinois, Chicago, believes that the obscenity laws that are already in existence inhibit First Amendment rights.

*The very fact that obscenity laws exist legitimizes the concept that a commission, legislature, or court is empowered with the wisdom and with the au-*

*Al Goldstein, also known as the
"Prince of Porn," in his Manhattan office*

*thority to prevent other people from reading or viewing what they wish. That concept creates a clear and present danger to a free society. Today it legitimizes the suppression of explicit sexual material—but it wasn't always that in the past and it won't always be that in the future; it will be something else—whatever society at a given time finds "offensive." This is a basic rejection of democracy. Democracy assumes that individuals are capable of selecting what they wish to read, that they are capable of selecting from among the myriad religious, social, political, and other ideas. Anything less is a rejection of the most basic assumption in our society: that citizens are capable of making decisions for themselves.*[6]

In the next chapter, we will examine some alliances between unlikely groups of people—people who have little in common other than a desire to prohibit the making, selling, or showing of pornography.

# UNLIKELY
# ALLIANCES

Pornography is an emotional issue that may sometimes conflict with peoples' sense of decency, religious views, or ideas of personal freedom. One person's religious belief that obscene material be limited or outlawed can interfere with another person's demand for free speech.

Disagreements about pornography have split old alliances and created new ones; alliances have been formed between groups of people that previously had not had much, if anything, in common.

Some anti-porn feminists, who had garnered support from liberals, who encouraged open discussion on new or progressive ideas, now find themselves in league with right-wing conservatives and fundamentalist religious leaders.

Feminists who oppose pornography first began to speak out in 1976 when a billboard appeared in Los Angeles promoting a record album. It pictured a bound and bruised woman with the caption, "I'm Black and Blue from the Rolling Stones—and I Love It!"[1]

Like Andrea Dworkin and Catharine MacKinnon, who wrote the controversial Minneapolis ordinance, many feminists link pornography to women's rights. "The image of male dominance is . . . at the root of all forms of sexual violence," said Beth Ann Carey, a United Methodist minister who spoke at a pornography conference sponsored by conservative groups and the United Methodist Church. As reported in the January 16, 1986, issue of *Christianity Today*, she continued, "Creating and keeping a system of inequality is where we, the church, have invited pornography and sexual violence to come sit in our sanctuaries."

The problem that antiporn feminists now face is how to voice their disapproval of porn without looking prudish or becoming too closely allied with the conservative right, which has traditionally disagreed with feminist goals. Some feminists have stated that they are not concerned with who their allies are now or who they have been in the past. They feel that it is important for all people who deplore the subjugation of women depicted in pornography to unite and voice their concerns.

The pornography issue has split feminist groups around the country. Many women feel that tampering with First Amendment rights would be detrimental to their cause. After all, they say, if pornographers' right to free speech is limited, maybe the free speech of feminists will be curtailed at some time in the future. Burton Joseph, a lawyer for *Playboy*, says, "Many feminists who favor this approach forget that censorship is always directed at lifestyle dissidents—the ultimate victims are going to be the people who support this method." But Catharine MacKinnon disagrees, pointing out that the law can be narrowly interpreted. She thinks that even though some people might abuse it, that should not be grounds for gutting it.[2]

Law enforcement officials have joined feminists in antiporn activities, largely because of pornography's link to organized crime. Assistant Attorney General Lois Herrington of the U.S. Justice Department was quoted in the October 1985 issue of *Ladies' Home Journal* as saying, ". . . analyses in Cleveland, Los Angeles and Phoenix have shown that sex crimes are higher in those areas where hard-core pornography is available." These analyses, however, do not prove that pornography is the cause of the violence.

The conservative religious community finds itself in agreement with feminists on the pornography issue and is speaking out. Dr. Harry Hollis, a Baptist minister and ethicist, works for the Christian Life Commission of the Southern Baptist Convention. He says,

> *One of pornography's worst sins is the way it serves to generate hostility instead of fellowship between the sexes, exploitation instead of love. . . . Its major harm is not that it tells too much about sex, but that it tells too little. It conveys the idea that a male and a female are the sum of their private parts. Sexuality is more than a one-dimensional force.*[3]

Joining the feminists and religious leaders are numerous other groups of citizens who strongly oppose pornography. One such group is the Parents Music Resource Center, headed by Tipper Gore, wife of Democratic Senator Albert Gore, Jr., of Tennessee. This group became well-known for a successful letter-writing campaign in which they persuaded recording companies to label their records if they contained objectionable language.[4]

Political and social conservatives have joined the call for laws against porn. To many people, it seems ironic that conservatives, who traditionally support measures

*Townspeople in West Haven, Connecticut,
demonstrate near an empty building
intended as the site of a porn shop.*

that "get the government off the backs" of the American people, are now demanding that laws be passed to curtail pornography, laws which, in effect, intrude on the privacy of individuals.

Conservatives answer that they, along with many other mainstream Americans, are simply reacting to what they believe is a deplorable breakdown in traditional family values. They say that they are a part of the country's swing back to the right.

Conservative religious leader, Reverend Jerry Falwell, agrees with this philosophy. In a *Time* magazine article July 21, 1986, Falwell says,

> *The new moralism in this country has been growing for the past two decades. The awakening is manifesting itself in the change in the national lifestyle. . . . We recognize the existence of pornography and the impossibility of stamping it all out. But we do want to push it back to Sleaze Town to live amongst the roaches where it belongs.*

Falwell believes that President Reagan's conservative politics have served as both cause and effect of the country's new morality. "The country is moving politically to the right, and Ronald Reagan is a product of that phenomenon. He has been produced by it and has contributed to it."[5]

Because it has been so difficult to define obscenity and prove material obscene, the attitude among some government officials is not to waste time bringing pornographers to court. *Newsweek* (March 18, 1985), reported that former Attorney General William French Smith disagreed with some conservatives who, early in Reagan's presidency, wanted to form a prosecution task force against pornographers. Instead, he instructed the FBI and U.S. attorneys to direct their efforts to child porn and organized crime's involvement in the selling and distribution of pornography.

On the local level antipornography leaders also have found that attacking a narrow segment of pornography is more successful than waging an all-out war on porn in general. Church of God secretary, Paul Tanner, advises focusing on "removing all pornography which involves or affects children, and pornography which depicts the graphic, sexually explicit subordination and degradation of women." In a January 17, 1986, article in *Christianity Today*, Tanner says he is aware this narrow focus will not satisfy everyone, but he maintains it is necessary in order to broaden their base of support.

In the political arena, on both the local and national levels, the Democrats and the Republicans are interested in winning as many of the votes of the so-called "baby boomers" as possible. ("Baby boomers" is a name given to the large group of babies born between the end of World War II and the mid-1960s.)

"The key word for 1988 is tolerance," says Roger Stone, a Republican strategist. George Bush's strategist, Lee Atwater, maintains that whoever wins the 1988 election will have to be politically similar to Ronald Reagan. "Reagan won the baby-boom vote in 1984 because he projected tolerance. They did not think that Reagan would impose his personal views on them. A Republican can afford to be more conservative on social issues as long as he conveys the notion of tolerance."[6]

*St. Louis County Sheriff Harold Hoeh loading a box with copies of* The Happy Hooker *into a police car after seizing them from a bookstore. In 1973, under a court order, the book, an autobiography of a former prostitute, was declared to be obscene. It was judged to be without any redeeming social value.*

—42

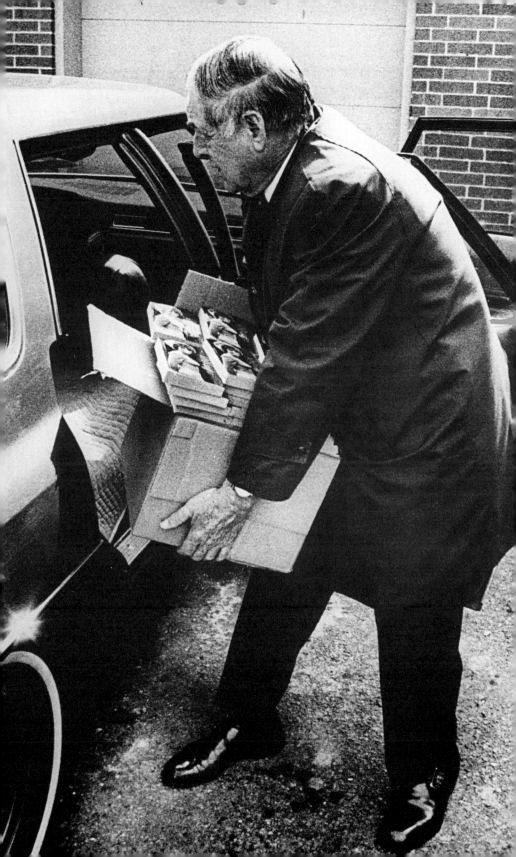

Seka

A Senate Judiciary subcommittee on pornography was considering possible legislative responses to porn. This "adult film" actress testified that she believed the government should have stiffer penalties for child pornographers.

As writer Richard Stengel of *Time* has pointed out (July 21, 1986), tolerance is a word that is not heard often from people involved in a crusade. But in the controversy over sexual freedom, people who do not employ some tolerance do so at their own risk. Stengel reminds us that history has shown that whenever "moral fervor held sway," there was always a resulting counter-response where individual liberties were threatened. And so, he warns political and social leaders to beware of carrying their "moral" zeal too far. They may be "left stranded when the pendulum swings the other way. And it always does."

# PORNOGRAPHY
# AND RELIGION

Some of pornography's most vocal critics are religious leaders, some of whom view pornographic material as contributing to the increase of sexually active youths, teen pregnancies, and the breakdown in family values.

Kenneth S. Kantzer, in an April 17, 1987, editorial in *Christianity Today*, wrote about his concern that young people today are receiving their sex education from pornographic material. He cites statistics provided by Henry Boatwright, chairman of the U.S. Advisory Board for Social Concerns, indicating that 70 percent of all pornographic magazines are read by minors. One member of his group estimated that the audience for hard-core porn consists of males from fifteen to nineteen.

Kantzer warns his readers that those who support pornographers portray those opposed to it as "narrow-minded religious bigots, ultraconservative in their attitudes toward life, hopelessly outdated, and determined to destroy freedom of speech and freedom of press in all other areas of American life."

Kantzer calls for concerned people to take four necessary steps to fight pornography's influence: one, teach sex education at home and in church-sponsored youth groups; two, voice objections to pornography at parent-teacher meetings and wherever books and magazines are sold; three, support others who are fighting porn through petition drives and boycotts of stores that sell or display porn; and fourth, encourage studies that educate people and give them a clear understanding of the difference between opposition to pornography and opposition to freedom of speech. Many people, he says, do not understand the definition of obscenity.

Another editorial in *Christianity Today*, dated February 19, 1982, suggests that Christians who disagree with what they see on network television, cable, or radio should complain to the Federal Communications Commission.

Some religious groups pushing for a crackdown on pornography attempt to educate their members. A January 1, 1982, article in *Christianity Today* reported on a conference of church leaders, legislators, and law enforcement officials that was held to discuss the problem of pornography. A local sponsor of the conference was the Citizens for Decency through Law which is based in Phoenix.

The article, "Why People Don't Fight Porn," listed a number of reasons outlined by the conference leaders to explain why people seem apathetic about the problem. Here are their reasons:

1. Ignorance about how vicious pornography has become. Many people, the conference leaders say, are unaware that pornographic materials are not simply the "naughty

magazines" of past generations, but their pages (and now videos) have come to be filled with group sex, bestiality, masturbation, rape, and sexual assault, and even sex murders.

2. Ignorance of the ways that pornography influences its readers. Salt Lake City psychologist Victor Cline reported to conference members that like addictive drugs, pornography users have shown a need for exposure to more and more violent pornography and that users tend to act out the fantasies about which they have read.

3. Peoples' defensiveness about the idea that "you can't legislate morality." Laws are not written to change the minds of individuals, the conference leaders say, but to prevent people from succumbing to greed, lust, hate, or rage in ways that could harm others.

4. The popular belief that there is no room for censorship in a democratic society. But conference leaders say that the public has the right to pass laws that will protect their quality of life.

5. The belief that the public has no right to curb "victimless crime among consenting adults."

Conference leaders say that the participants as well as the public are being victimized. The conference leaders then reviewed what is and is not legal in the eyes of the Supreme Court because they felt one reason for society's lack of concern is the confusion over what is and is not permitted by the Constitution.

Conference participants concluded that there are two steps that should be taken to curb the pornography industry. First, citizens should encourage law enforcement at the national level to eliminate existing porn and halt any new forms of porn in the beginning stages. Second, they should appeal to President Reagan's administration to require the Federal Communications Commission to regulate what can be shown on cable television. (The FCC had remained uninvolved with this issue in the past, saying that cable TV does not use the airwaves and so is not under its jurisdiction.)

Conservative Christian leaders have been joined by others in their fight against pornography. One of the best known groups is the National Federation for Decency (NFD), headquartered in Tupelo, Mississippi. It boasts 350 chapters across the country. The NFD publishes a journal that reports on social and religious issues of interest to its readers. One major focus of the journal is news regarding what is being done at the local and national level to fight pornography.

One of the functions of the *NFD Journal* is to keep tabs on businesses that display pornography or sponsor television programs that contain offensive language or subject matter judged to be unacceptable by the NFD. A cover story of the March 1987 issue of the *NFD Journal* announced nationwide picketing of Holiday Inns because the hotel chain offers adult sex movies to visitors in their rooms. The article described how several NFD supporters checked into a Holiday Inn to see whether the hotel was still offering offensive movies. The article then listed eight sex movies available and graphically described the most offensive scenes in one of the movies.

The *NFD Journal* also reviews movies and television programs deemed unsuitable because of "crude and/or suggestive dialogue; illegal drug use/alcohol drinking; homosexual conduct; crude or rough language; nudity; near nudity; other (occult, defying authority, etc.); profanity (taking God's name in vain); sexual intercourse implied or obscured; sexual intercourse shown; violence." In the May/June 1987 issue, the *Journal* took issue with a situation comedy program it found to be unacceptable. In the article titled "Teen sex urged by family series" and subtitled "J.C. Penney, ABC family show approve premarital sex," the *NFD Journal* describes a recent episode of "Growing Pains": "The April 7 episode of "Growing Pains" had the psychiatrist-father give his stamp of approval to pre-marital sex as he told his ten-year-old that people have sex when 'they care about each other.' The episode was written by Tim O'Donnell and directed by John Tracy. . . . No marriage, no commitment of any sort—just 'caring' about each other at the moment." Then the article named several of the advertisers of the program, gave the advertisers' addresses (so that readers could send complaints), and listed products promoted in the advertisements (so that readers might protest by refusing to buy those products).

The boycotts that the *NFD Journal* encourages have been very successful in removing porn from the shelves of convenience stores. "Free speech does not mean it is free of consequences," says Andrea Vangor in a March 18, 1985, article in *Newsweek* magazine. Vangor organized a boycott of convenience stores in Seattle that stocked *Penthouse* magazine.

One of the most successful boycott efforts caused Southland Corporation, owner of 7-Eleven stores, to remove *Playboy, Penthouse*, and *Forum* magazines from their shelves in April 1986. Southland also urged its 3,600 franchises to do the same. The 7-Eleven stores had been boycotted and picketed by supporters of the National Federation for Decency and the Rev. Jerry Falwell's Liberty Federation.

Jere Thompson, president of Southland, said his company was responding to hearings that had been conducted by the Federal Commission on Pornography in which, he said, "The testimony indicates a growing public awareness of a possible connection between adult magazines and crime, violence and child abuse."

An editorial, published in *Christianity Today* (June 27, 1980), says that many Christians do not become involved in the fight against pornography because they feel they should show tolerance.

Members of the National
Federation for Decency picket
outside an ABC television
affiliate station in Houston.
They were promoting a viewers'
boycott of ABC in an attempt to
get sex and violence off TV.

*But for the sake of our entire social structure, tol- eration must be limited or we destroy ourselves as people. Murder or theft, if tolerated, would destroy the structure of human society. But the morally sen- sitive person recognizes that in the long run por- nography is more devastating to society than theft. Stealing robs us of things; pornography robs us of character. Stealing destroys property; pornography destroys our humanity. In a fallen and sinful so- ciety, we cannot expect to be freed from the tension of drawing hard lines between toleration and so- cially destructive permissiveness.*

This editorial writer also argues with those who use the First Amendment to the Constitution in defense of pornography.

*The purveyor of pornography does not seek to com- municate his own ideas and convictions so as to share them with others or to convince others of the truth; he is simply without conscience, selling for profit material that he would not like his own chil- dren to use. Wise laws against pornography do not inhibit the freedom to express ideas; they restrict profiteering aimed at the destruction of society.*

In a February 7, 1986, editorial in *Christianity Today*, Kenneth Kantzer uses the argument that pornography is condemned in the Bible, not as pornography per se, but in general. ". . . the whole Bible condemns lust and lewd- ness," he writes. Kantzer stresses that sex is a gift from God, that our bodies were intended for procreation and enjoyment. But, he writes, the *obsession* with sex is what is harmful, and he quotes Jesus in his Sermon on the Mount: "But I tell you that anyone who looks at a woman lustfully has already committed adultery with her in his heart."

Kantzer then cites the pattern of behavior of pornography users that was outlined in a psychology study at the University of Utah by Professor Victor Cline:

1. *Addiction.* Cline's study shows that porn users, like drug abusers, need more and more pornographic material to get a sexual "high."

2. *Escalation.* Also like the drug user, the porn user needs increasingly graphic and "usually more brutalizing levels of stimulation."

3. *Desensitization.* After reading porn, readers tend to become used to its effects; that what was, at first, shocking and disgusting, becomes to the reader commonplace, and the pain or humiliation of another person becomes unimportant.

4. *Acting out.* Pornographic materials have served, in effect, as how-to manuals, so that readers view porn and then act out what they have ["learned."]

Many churches have felt a need to compose statements directed to their members about their official stand on pornography. One such statement was written in 1974 by the Seventeenth General Convention of the American Lutheran Church. The statement is included in an interesting book about pornography called *Pornography and Sexual Violence* by Gary E. McCuen. This statement regarding pornography was to be used by local churches as an aid to decisions and actions.

The first point in "A Christian Perspective on Pornography" addresses the word "obscene." Pornography, the statement says, may be obscene, but so are other words and actions, such as war, hate, violence, human exploitation, and making material interests have greater worth than human values. The statement warns Christians to be careful not to express disapproval only of sexual obscenities.

The statement to Lutherans raises a number of questions about pornography that the members of the General Convention felt should be considered by thoughtful Christians:

*Is it either right, necessary, or salutary to use civil laws to set standards for thoughts, tastes, and attitudes toward sexual practices?*

*How can persons and communities be protected against sex-saturated materials and outlets which offend the sensitive or exploit the gullible?*

*What room is there, with both freedom and responsibility, to explore issues and problems in human sexuality even though they run counter to current taboos and standards?*

*Why is so much of the sexual relegated to the realm of the forbidden and why is it made so difficult for people to appreciate their sexual selves and their sexual feelings?*

*How does the Gospel liberate the believer from crippling enslavement both to prevailing sexual stereotypes and to self-centered pursuit of erotic pleasures?*

The statement also summarizes the then prevailing legal attitude about pornography as published in the 1970 Report of the Commission on Obscenity and Pornography.

*New York's Cardinal John J. O'Connor on the steps of St. Patrick's Cathedral where he led a meeting of prominent religious leaders in a battle against pornography*

The report advocated the right of consenting adults to read, obtain, or view sexually explicit material, but also recommended that the sale of porn to minors be regulated and suggested that legislation be adopted that would prevent those who disapprove of porn from having it thrust upon them. (We will take a closer look at the 1970 report in the following chapter.)

The statement reviews several decisions by the Supreme Court in 1973 that reaffirmed its earlier position, that obscene material was not protected by the First Amendment.

Then church members are asked to consider that since pornography exists as a business, the best way to attack it is simply to refuse to buy it and to set good examples for young people in reading and viewing choices.

Freedom, the statement says, gives us opportunities to grow spiritually. Pornography and the freedom to choose gives us the opportunity to "grow in understanding and appreciation for God's gift of human sexuality."

As we have seen, religious leaders have not hesitated to take a stand against pornography. The argument that most religious leaders make against pornography is the highly publicized link between obscenity and violence.

In Harry Genet's January 1, 1982 editorial in *Christianity Today*, he quotes the founder of Citizens for Decency through Law, Charles H. Keating, Jr., who cited the following statistics: police vice squads report that "77 percent of child molesters of boys and 87 percent of child molesters of girls admitted imitating the sexual behavior they had seen modeled in pornography." Keating also points to a Michigan State police detective who studied sexual assault cases from 1956 through 1979. Of those 38,000 episodes, 41 percent involved the use of pornography either just before or during the attack. While a causal relationship has not been proven here, antiporn activists use these statistics in their attempt to convince the public that porn is dangerous.

The relationship between pornography and violence has become an important issue, not only to religious leaders, but also to lawmakers, politicians, psychologists, and concerned citizens. In the next chapter, we will examine the porn-violence link and see what the experts have to say.

# PORNOGRAPHY
# AND VIOLENCE

Most antiporn activists agree that the best and most effective argument against pornographic material would be evidence that porn and violence are linked.

While some pornography contains no violent images, others depict graphic violence. Whippings, beatings, mutilation, rape, and even murder on film (so-called "snuff" films) are a part of today's pornography scene.

But violence is not limited to hard-core pornography. Sexual images are used frequently in advertising, and some suggest violent acts with varying degrees of aggression. Advertisements sometimes use sado-masochism (S&M). This term refers to sadistic and masochistic behaviors where someone obtains sexual pleasure from mistreating or hurting another person or from being mistreated or hurt.

Young people may not be consciously aware of it, but many of the rock videos shown on video cable stations in effect "sell" sexual violence by showing young men or women scantily dressed and carrying whips or chains, while the lyrics suggest anger toward someone of the opposite sex.

Rape is a serious problem in the United States. Many women are afraid to go out alone, particularly at night, and with good reason. Every eight minutes someone is raped in this country, and most of the victims are women.

Could pornography and the pervasiveness of sexual violence when shown on the large and small screen and in magazines and books have a *causal* relationship to the growing number of sexual attacks upon women in the United States? There is no definitive answer to this question.

This question was studied by the national Commission on Obscenity and Pornography in 1970. The commission did not link porn and violence.

*Surveys of psychiatrists, psychologists, sex educators, social workers, counselors and similar professional workers reveal that large majorities of such groups believe that sexual materials do not have harmful effects on either adults or adolescents. . . . A study of a heterogeneous group of young people found that exposure to erotica had no impact upon moral character over and above that of a generally deviant background.*

*In sum, empirical research designed to clarify the question has found no evidence to date that exposure to explicit sexual materials plays a significant role in the causation of delinquent or criminal behavior among youth or adults. The Commission cannot conclude that exposure to erotic materials is a factor in the causation of sex crime or sex delinquency.*

Many people, including some psychologists, believe that men commit acts of sexual aggression and rape out of a need to overpower and dominate, not out of a sexual desire for the victim.

Dr. Helen Tiahrt, a staff psychologist at the Mount Pleasant Correctional Facility, which treats sex offenders from the state of Iowa, says,

> *In rape cases . . . so many people think the cause of rape is sexual drive, and it isn't that very often. It's not uncommon for rapists to get out of bed with their wives or lovers and go out and rape someone. They're power rapists, not oversexed. With low self-esteem, they feel as though somebody else is controlling them, that their whole life is being controlled. Sex is the way they act out their power.*

According to Dr. Tiahrt, most men with whom she works at the facility choose weak victims.

One of the staff counselors at Mount Pleasant, Sherry Roffe, says that most of the men she works with insist that pornography was not involved in their crimes. But another counselor on the staff, Ron Mullen, says that pornography can play a part in what he calls "the deviant cycle." This is where the offender begins the cycle by viewing pornographic material and ends in molesting or raping someone.

Catharine MacKinnon, who cowrote the Minneapolis ordinance against pornography, has said that porn "eroticizes dominance and submission, of which rape, battery, sexual harassment, and the sexual and physical abuse of children are also forms of practice."

Susan Griffin, in her book, *Pornography and Silence: Culture's Revenge Against Nature*, goes a step further. She says that pornography is, in effect, propaganda that teaches men that sex has nothing to do with emotions.

Amy Elman, a member of Women Against Pornography, in an interview for *Ladies' Home Journal* (October 1985), commented that pornographic books and movies make it look as if women's purpose is to make their bodies available to men. "Men want us to do what they see in the magazines. They put pressure on us and why not? Pornographic magazines are manuals for sexual abuse."

The same issue of *Ladies' Home Journal* reported that some social science experts are convinced that porn can cause or inspire crimes against women: "Assistant Attorney General Lois Herrington, of the U.S. Department of Justice, has stated that 'analyses in Cleveland, Los Angeles and Phoenix have shown that sex crimes are higher in those areas where hard-core pornography is available.' " While this fact does not prove a cause-and-effect relationship, it is the kind of information used by antiporn activists to persuade others to accept their point of view.

In 1985, Senator Arlen Specter (Republican of Pennsylvania), who was a member of a congressional subcommittee that studied the effects of pornography, announced that the testimony he had heard "provides substantial evidence that many individuals are forced to perform sexual acts suggested by pornographic materials and suffer harm as a result."

Other experts who have studied the link between pornography and violence say any cause-and-effect conclusions are not clear-cut. One is Edward Donnerstein, a psychologist in the Center for Communication Research in the communication arts department at the University of Wisconsin. His investigation, conducted with his partner, Daniel Linz, a member of the psychology department at the University, was first published in *Psychology Today*, and reprinted in Gary E. McCuen's book, *Pornography and Sexual Violence*. Donnerstein points out that researchers had already shown that exposure to as little as

several minutes of sexually violent pornography (a depiction of rape, for instance) can "increase the viewer's acceptance of rape myths (for example, that women want to be raped), increase aggressive behavior against women in a laboratory setting and decrease one's sensitivity to rape and the plight of the rape victim."

Donnerstein wanted to know whether the viewing of films that depicted violence toward women would "spill over" and affect other attitudes about the women. Male subjects were asked to watch nearly ten hours of commercial films that were sexually violent toward women. The men watched five films, one every day for five consecutive days. They saw either R-rated movies such as *Tool Box Murders, Vice Squad, I Spit on Your Grave*, and *Texas Chainsaw Massacre*; X-rated movies that showed sexually explicit scenes between consenting adults; or X-rated films showing sexual assault.

After the men watched the ten hours of films, they were asked to fill out a questionnaire about their moods and to evaluate the films they had seen. There were several groups of men in the study, and the groups saw the films in different order so that researchers could compare the attitudes about the same films and how they were evaluated on the first and the last day of viewing.

After their week of viewing films, the men were asked to watch another film, this one reenacting a true-life rape trial. Then the subjects were asked to decide how responsible the woman was for the crime inflicted upon her and to what extent she suffered injury.

Donnerstein was particularly interested in the results of the group that watched the R-rated films graphically depicting violence toward women. After the first day of watching these films, the men indicated on the question-

*Waging war against pornography*

naire that they were significantly more depressed, more anxious, and more annoyed than normal. However, on each succeeding day of the study, their scores changed, until by the end of the fourth day, their moods were back to where they started. The results made Donnerstein ask, "What had happened to the viewers as they watched more and more violence?"

Donnerstein's conclusion was that the men were being *desensitized* to the violence. In other words, as they viewed more and more violence, they were less emotionally affected by it, and they came to accept it more.

On the first day, the men reported that they had seen four "offensive scenes." By day five, they reported only two, even though they had viewed the exact same movies, only in reverse order.

Donnerstein said, "Most startling, by the last day of viewing graphic violence against women, the men were rating the material as significantly less debasing and degrading to women, more humorous and more enjoyable, and they claimed a greater willingness to see this type of film again."

Donnerstein reported that two films in particular illustrated the changes in attitudes among the men studied. Both of the films, *I Spit on Your Grave* and *Vice Squad*, contain scenes depicting sexual assault, but the former is quite graphic and the latter more ambiguous. The men who first saw *Vice Squad* and then *I Spit on Your Grave* rated the two movies as equal in violent content. "However, subjects who had seen the more graphic movie first saw much less sexual violence (rape) in the more ambiguous film," according to Donnerstein.

When the subjects watched the film of the reenacted rape trial, Donnerstein reported, "The victim of rape was rated as significantly more worthless and her injury as significantly less severe by those men who had been exposed to filmed violence than by a control group who saw only the rape trial and did not view any of our films."

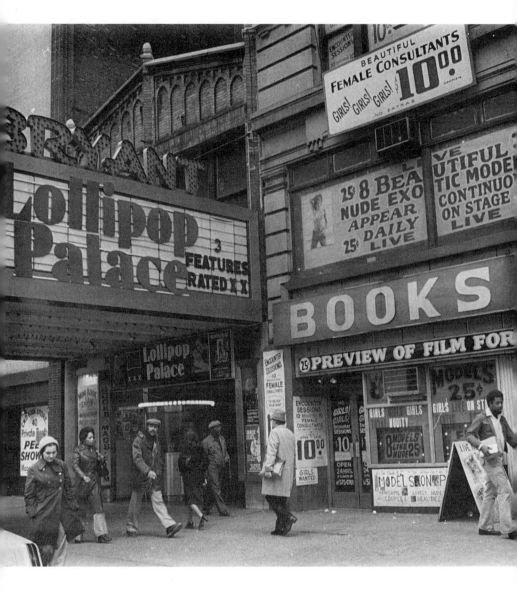

*Many people believe pornographic films and books desensitize men in their attitudes toward women.*

Donnerstein indicated in his *Psychology Today* article that he would continue to study the desensitizing effects of violent films. He also wrote that he and his associates would be studying in a laboratory environment how those films might affect aggression toward women and how nonviolent films, such as *Porky's*, which portray women as nothing more than sex objects, affect the attitudes of men viewers about women in general.

These researchers did not send their subjects back "out into the world" without extensive debriefing. This consisted of sessions with the researchers and videotaped programs that, in effect, "resensitized" the men, particularly to dispel the rape myth (that women like to be raped) and to help instill the men's original discomfort with the violence displayed toward women.

Donnerstein reports that these sessions were productive, and he expressed an interest in exploring how effective these sessions might be in influencing the attitudes of subjects if they occurred *before* the films were viewed. "If this proves to be effective," Donnerstein said, "it might eventually be advisable to package sexually violent films with a warning that would help counter the negative effects of exposure to mass-media sexual violence."

Marcia Pally, a writer who takes an anticensorship stand in a June 29, 1985 issue of the *Nation*, questions Donnerstein's conclusions:

> *There are . . . questions to be asked of this research. Show a male college sophomore a series of pornographic films that include rape and he might evince decreased sensitivity to rape victims in a post-screening questionnaire or mock trial. But could the subject's knowledge that his scores will be compared with those of other college men produce a "sexual bravura" skew in his answers? Does the subject's familiarity with the goals of his professor's study predetermine useful responses? (Most of this research was done with psychology students partic-*

*ipating for extra credit.) Is watching blue movies in a laboratory the same as viewing it at home or in a 42nd Street booth? Could "desensitization" to on-screen violence be boredom or the normal response to the familiar? Donnerstein has pointed out that doctors in emergency rooms don't faint at the sight of each new bloody body, but that hardly means they're going to commit murder.*

Catharine MacKinnon is concerned with the amount of sexual violence depicted in ads, movies, and television. She wrote a position paper for the Minneapolis City Council in December 1983, in defense of her proposed city ordinance against pornography. (This paper is published in part in Gary E. McCuen's book, *Pornography and Sexual Violence*.) MacKinnon wrote, "Given the pervasiveness of the abuses [in pornography], . . . it can not be seen as a corrupt and confused misrepresentation of what is otherwise a natural, healthy sexual situation. It is not a distortion, a reflection, a projection, an expression, or a symbol either. It is the sexuality of the male supremacy. . . ."

MacKinnon is concerned that pornography suggests that women *want* to be "battered and raped and sexually harassed." She says that pornography allows men to put women into the roles and situations that they (the men) desire, such as the sufferers of rape, torture, humiliation, and even death. "I have to conclude that this is erotic to the male standpoint. . . . We are in pornography to be violated."

MacKinnon says that often pornography is portrayed as the liberator of human sexuality, but, she says, from the feminist point of view, "it is a defense not only of force, of the sexual terrorism of rape, but of the subordination of women to men clear and simple. In this sense, sexual liberation means freeing male sexual aggression. What in the defense of pornography is called love and romance, in the feminist viewpoint is hatred. What in the

*Marches against porn have taken place all across the nation. This one was held in San Francisco.*

defense of pornography is called pleasure and eroticism, in the feminist perspective is violation. What they call desire, we call lust for dominance and submission."

Aryeh Neier, former national executive director of the American Civil Liberties Union, does not believe that pornography causes violence toward women. He says,

*For a good many years, I confronted the issue of pornography as a civil libertarian, defending the right of anyone to express himself in any way he chose as long as he did not directly infringe on the rights of others. Since I left the American Civil Liberties Union six years ago, I've worked for organizations that are concerned with human rights in various repressive countries. In these countries, whether they are in Central America or Africa or Eastern Europe or wherever, there is virtually no pornography; but there is a great deal of the same hostility toward women and the same violence against women that one finds in the United States. In fact, in many of these countries sexual violence— mass rape or sexual torture or sexual humiliation— is one of the main forms political repression takes. I conclude from the astounding level of sexual violence in these countries and the absence of pornography that pornography is really not very important, that it is no more or less important than the great variety of images that dominates the media in the United States and other Western countries: images of sex and violence and melodrama and ugliness and beauty.*

Harold M. Voth, M.D., a faculty member at the Karl Menninger School of Psychiatry in Topeka, Kansas, wrote an article published in the March 1987 issue of the National Federation for Decency in which he addressed what he thinks are some of the psychological and social effects of pornography. He wrote:

—69

*If one is exposed to an environmental stimulus (situation or experience) which is similar or identical in form or meaning, or both, to an earlier one which has been repressed into the deeper regions of the mind (the subconscious), the latter will be triggered, activated and mobilized and will influence the individual to some degree. Obviously, the strength of the external stimulus and the "quantity" of the repressed mental content and the depth to which it has been repressed will determine the extent to which the latter affects conscious mental life.*

Voth went on to observe: "Viewing pornography, most of which depicts perverse behavior, activates the developmental sexual arrests which exist in millions of people. Now then, reflect on the enormous impact the pornography industry is having on the values, feelings, behavioral standards, and the mental health of massive numbers of people who are exposed to these pathological stimuli. Furthermore, these persons whose prurient appeal is aroused seem to develop a kind of addiction for pornography and, therefore, receive many exposures over time."

The July 1987 issue of the National Federation for Decency *Journal* and a March 1986 article in *Christianity Today* both include interesting information about a study that indicates that people who see nonviolent pornography tend to go on to read the violent porn. Dolf Zillman at the University of Indiana and Dennings Bryant of the University of Houston conducted the research. One hundred-and-sixty randomly selected adults and college students from the University of Indiana at Bloomington were asked to view either one hour of nonviolent X-rated movies with sexual scenes or prime-time situation-comedies during a one-hour session, once a week for six weeks. At the end of that time, the group that had watched the nonviolent pornography tended, in general, to choose violence and bestiality, and even avoided the nonviolent porn. The researchers' conclusion, as stated in the National Federation of Decency *Journal*, is that their findings "strongly support the view that continued exposure to non-violent heterosexual pornography arouses interest in and creates a taste for porn that portrays less commonly practiced sexual activities, including those involving the infliction of pain."

Another of their findings was that men began to think of women as sexual playthings, became more sexually aggressive, and began to think of rape as a trivial matter. Subjects also tended to believe in the rape myth—that all women secretly want to be raped. Dolf was reported to say in the *Christianity Today* article, "There can be no doubt that pornography, as a form of primarily male entertainment, promotes the victimization of women."

There are social scientists who believe that the factors that shape a person's attitudes about sex have done their work long before the individual has been exposed to pornography. These scientists believe that the use of porn is simply a *symptom* of a deep-seated disturbance, and not the *cause* of sexual deviancy.

Edward Donnerstein, of the University of Wisconsin, for example, is more concerned with the presence of violence in the media than with the presence of nonviolent porn.

In the *Time* July 21, 1986 article, he comments that violent movies such as *Rambo* affect the attitudes of people the same way that violent porn does. "If you take out the sex and leave the violence, you get the increased violent behavior in the laboratory setting, and these 'changes in attitude.' If you take out the violence and leave the sex, nothing happens."

Sol Gordon, professor of child and family studies at Syracuse University, says, "There is absolutely no evidence of a causal relationship between pornography and sexual acting out. . . . You can always illustrate by single instances; you can always get an incidence. The newspa-

pers will always help. You may find one rapist, and they found pornography in his room. And that means that pornography caused it. They also found milk in his refrigerator!"

Writer and critic Marcia Pally has an interesting theory about why violent porn exists and what should be done about it. She writes in the June 29, 1985, issue of the *Nation*:

> *What we learn from porn, fantasies by and for men, is that men are both drawn to and terrified of women—not surprising in a society where women perform most of the child-care duties. In infancy the child needs mom and delights in her solicitude, yet fears her apparent omnipotence and rages at its dependence on her. (Girls, too, get angry and afraid, but there is an edge of fury men feel about women that women don't because, after all, women are "us.")*
>
> *If porn tells us of man's love/hate for women and suggests the psychological genesis of this ambivalence, perhaps women should seek to dismantle the arrangements that foster this love/hate rather than attack its representations. If men and women took care of children equally, we all would still have our memories of infancy and fear of dependence. But mom wouldn't be the sole focus of our expectations and ire, and the female figure wouldn't be the only reminder of our helplessness. In such a world, we might still have porn, but the tales and pictures might be less imbalanced, less sexist. . . .*

*Feminist groups believe that pornography destroys women's self images.*

—73

*Rather than closing porn parlors, we could spend our time better by getting mom out of the house, at least half the time, and getting dad back in. That would provide the double benefit of introducing more women to the public sphere (for independent incomes, political clout) and introducing dad to baby.*

It is important that informed citizens consider all the questions involved in the pornography issue, whether they be legal, religious, or moral. Basic questions of civil rights—those of people who do not want porn thrust upon them, as well as those who are alarmed at the idea of censorship in a democratic society—are at issue here. Only after considering all aspects of the controversy can we come to a decision about how the problems of pornography should be addressed.

# CHILD PORN

The most alarming development in the pornography industry is what has become known as "kiddie porn"—the harmful use of children as sex objects.

This type of pornography has flourished in recent years, spawning, according to *Christianity Today*, an estimated 275 monthly magazines devoted to the use of children in pornography.[1] Estimates vary as to how many children are involved in porn, but experts say there may be as many as one million children who have been sexually molested and photographed to create kiddie porn.[2]

Congress has concluded that much child pornography, as well as child prostitution, is a product of organized crime, and it operates on a nationwide scale. Kiddie porn production centers have been discovered in several large cities, such as New York, Chicago, and Los Angeles. But the industry is not limited to these areas. One of the difficult problems for law enforcement officials is that kiddie porn can be produced in private homes and is therefore very difficult to uncover.

Child porn is even more lucrative than porn that features adults. The profits are staggering. Although it may cost as little as 35 to 50 cents to produce each copy of a child porn magazine, it can be sold for from $7.50 up to $12.50.[3] It is also relatively inexpensive to buy home video equipment to produce a child porn film, which can be copied and sold for up to $200 a copy.[4]

As we have seen, many Americans believe in the right of adults to publish, distribute, and sell pornography to other adults. However, most people agree that there should be no place for porn that victimizes children.

Many of the children who appear in kiddie porn are runaways who have been picked up off the streets by people who want nothing more than to abuse them and make money off them. As many as one million young people run away from home every year. These youngsters are vulnerable to porn producers who find them at bus stations and fast food outlets and offer them food, money, or drugs in exchange for sexual favors.

Children exploited for pornography purposes range in age from less than a year to eighteen years of age. Victimized children have been photographed in nursery schools or by trusted "friends" of the family. Still others are kidnapped and molested by strangers before being photographed. Some children are exploited by their own parents who actually "rent" their children as child porn models.

A U.S. Senate committee report in 1981 drew up a profile of a typical young boy who might be sexually exploited:

*Between 8 and 17 years old;*

*An underachiever in school or at home;*

*Came from a home where the parents were absent either physically or psychologically;*

*Usually without previous homosexual experience;*

*Had no strong moral or religious obligations;*

*Usually had no record of previous delinquency;*

*Suffered from poor sociological development*[5]

Law enforcement officials have discovered that there is a link between sexual exploitation and child prostitution. Often, a person who hires a child prostitute will photograph the child and copy and sell the photos to porn distributors.

The producers and distributors of child porn frequently are organized into "sex rings." One such operation was described in testimony to the U.S. Senate Subcommittee on Juvenile Justice on November 5, 1981. (An excerpt appears in Gary E. McCuen's Book *Pornography and Sexual Violence.*)

*. . . a Tennessee minister who operated a home for wayward boys encouraged the boys to engage in orgies. He then filmed them with hidden cameras and sold the films. Also, he arranged for "sponsors" to come to the home and have sex with the boys.*

Many of the people involved in child porn are called "pedophiles." A pedophile is an adult who is not able to relate sexually to another adult and receives sexual pleasure from having relations with children. In many cases, these disturbed adults are both the readers or viewers and the producers of child porn.

Pedophiles come from all walks of life—they may be teachers, bankers, transients, truck drivers. They may come from any social class, ethnic background, or religious persuasion. Experts say that like criminals who attack adults sexually, the child sex offender tends to have little self-esteem. The child sex abuser does not understand or value an intimate relationship with another person. Many sex offenders may have themselves been victims of sexual abuse as children.

"Many of these people have an underlying bad feeling about sex," says Dudley Allison, director of Iowa's Mount Pleasant Correctional Facility for sex offenders. "They've been sexually abused as youngsters, and sex has not been pleasant for them at any time. To them, sex is dirty, sex isn't fun, it isn't something two people consent to and enjoy together."

One man in the Mount Pleasant facility, Jack Blount, is serving twenty-four years for sexual assault. He believes that pornography contributed to his criminal life. Blount characterizes porn as an addiction.

The experts at the Mount Pleasant facility say that like alcoholics, sex offenders are never "cured" of their sexual deviancy. ". . . It's a process. A continual thing. It's day to day."

The *Journal* published by the National Federation for Decency published an article in May/June 1987 by Dr. Shirley O'Brien, a professor in Child Development and Family Relations at the University of Arizona in Tucson. O'Brien studied eight child molesters. She reported her findings in a book called *Why They Did It: Stories of Eight Convicted Child Molesters*. She found that the four men who had attacked young girls had had unpleasant relationships with females in their childhood. They had not been able to get along with mothers, sisters, and female teachers. "However, . . . they could relate to young girls because the young girls accepted them just as they were without judging them." Pornography, says Dr. O'Brien, played a part in the crimes of Bert, a forty-seven-year-old serving time for having sex with a young boy. "Child pornography seemed to be the motivational catalyst that gave Bert permission to molest." He had seen pornographic pictures as a young boy of boys in sexual activities. Bert said, "I sort of gave myself permission to do those things because my own early experiences were pleasurable and the child pornography showed the same thing."

Although some kiddie porn is produced by nationwide distribution organizations, the producer often is much closer to home and is an acquaintance or friend of the child's family and has reason or "permission" to be in close proximity to the child. The attacker will often prey on a child who is particularly vulnerable or in need of special understanding or attention.

One case described in the April 1983 *Ladies' Home Journal* article was that of a fourteen-year-old girl who had just been diagnosed as a diabetic. The young lady was having difficulty adjusting to her condition and trying to cope with the usual problems of adolescence as well. She found the confidant she needed in a fifty-three-year-old family friend.

For more than a year, the man acted as a kind and sensitive listener. But one day, long after she had let down her guard, the man molested her and took sexual photographs. He convinced her the episode was her fault and warned her that if she told her parents, her father would try to kill him, and he (her father) would be sent to prison. It was only after her twelve-year-old sister was sexually molested by the man that the girl told her parents what had taken place.

Other molesters have blackmailed their victims after convincing them that they were responsible for the sexual encounter. The pornographer might threaten the child by saying, "You allowed me to take these pictures of you smiling at the camera. If you tell anyone about us having sex, I'll show these pictures to your parents. Then they will know you did it willingly." The children, terrified of their parents' anger, will keep the episodes a secret.

The long-term effects of encounters with pornographers and sexual abusers can be devastating. Some experts say that these children suffer some of the same symptoms as children who have been the victims of incest. These effects may include depression and guilt. Many of these victims grow up to abuse their own children because they have not had the benefit of a positive, loving role model. Abuse is all they have experienced in an adult-child relationship.

Many children who have been the victims of this kind of exploitation repress their feelings of rage and try to "escape" by using alcohol or drugs.

"Some of these youngsters never get back into the mainstream," says Dr. Frank Osanka, interviewed in the *Ladies' Home Journal.* Osanka is a nationally known specialist in the prevention of sexual exploitation of children. "By the time they are fourteen and no longer young and 'attractive' enough to pose, they have accepted the pornographer's brainwashing—that they are no good—and so they go on to a deviant lifestyle."

According to Dr. Osanka, such experiences usually influence the child's attitude about sex later in life. Not surprisingly, after the child is told by the pornographer that he or she is to blame for what has happened, the child grows up to feel responsible for the past. These children also frequently think that there is something "wrong" with them, that they were at fault.

"That conviction," Dr. Osanka says, "can lead to promiscuity, or it can cause some youngsters to grow up believing sex is bad." Others, the article goes on to explain, may simply divorce their emotional feelings from the sex act.

Maurice Barker, a psychotherapist from Montreal who has treated victims of child porn, says, "The girls come to dread a man's touch. The boys who have performed in homosexual photos or films become awkward with women."[6]

The effect on adult sexual feelings and how the victims feel about themselves are just two of the ways that such an experience can change lives. Another devastating effect is the *memory* of having posed for the sexual photographs that may have been taken years earlier. What if, a young person may wonder, the photos are still in existence? What if they should surface someday? Will the pornographer contact me someday and blackmail me? "One photograph can haunt a child for a lifetime," Dr. Osanka says.[7]

Most of the arguments siding with the child pornography industry come from people who deplore the existence of child porn, but are concerned with the threat of First Amendment rights. The American Civil Liberties Union (ACLU) has had representatives at many congressional hearings dealing with pornography and crime, including the 1977 hearings that dealt with child pornography.

Gary E. McCuen, in his book *Pornography and Sexual Violence*, includes testimony to the 1977 House Subcommittee from Heather Florence, a member of the ACLU's Communications Media Committee. She was careful in her statement to draw a distinction between child abuse "which is unlawful activity and the dissemination of printed or visual materials which is constitutionally protected."

Ms. Florence made it clear to the subcommittee that the ACLU finds the exploitation of children for any reason to be worthy of condemnation. She urged the passage of strict laws that would prohibit child abuse in many forms, the private and commercial sexual abuse of children being one of them.

But she stressed that child pornography must not be attacked from the standpoint of the First Amendment. She said, ". . . while it is perfectly proper to prosecute those who engage in illegal action, constitutionally protected speech cannot be the vehicle." She said that the ACLU's position was that the people who *produce* the child pornography should be prosecuted for breaking the law. These people include those who recruit the children, take part in the sexual activities, or take the photographs. However, Florence says, ". . . those who have not participated in causing or engaging in the sexual activity but who may profit as a result of it, such as a publisher, editor, distributor or retailer, are not violating the law. While we may vigorously dislike and reject what they do, their activities in publishing and disseminating printed or visual materials are wholly protected by the First Amendment."

Many Americans think the ACLU's arguments here are not convincing. After all, they point out, not *all* printed material is legal. Libel laws make it illegal for publishers to print damaging lies about people. So why, they ask, should the First Amendment argument be used to protect child pornographers?

Most people, even those associated with the production of adult porn, are angered with the proliferation of child porn. Joe Steinman, who is chairman of the Essex Group, an adult porn conglomerate, says, "This is a monstrous crime. It bears no similarity to adult media, which features consenting people of legal age. Children don't have a choice—they're exploited."[8] He added that the Adult Film Association, an organization of which he is

*Child pornography has few supporters, even among those who feel porn shouldn't be outlawed.*

PEEP SHOWS
•36 MOVIES
•NEW MOVIES
WEEKLY
PRIVATE VIEWING BOOTHS
25¢
25¢
WE WON'T
OLERATE
CHILD PORNO

vice president, voted unanimously to throw out any member who involves himself in child pornography.

If there are so many people, even in the porn industry, who are outraged that child porn is available, why then does it still exist?

Father Bruce Ritter, who is founder of Covenant House, a nonprofit youth shelter in New York, says, "This sickness exists because a small segment of society wants it, another segment profits by it, and the rest aren't doing anything about it. Maybe we don't know enough—or care enough."9

Child porn has a surprising foe in Larry Flynt, the publisher of *Hustler* magazine, whose business is producing and selling pornography. He testified before the House Subcommittee on Crime in 1977 about his concern that child porn is attacked with the wrong argument—the First Amendment. Flynt no doubt realizes that any success in curbing child porn using the First Amendment argument (that pornography—here, child porn—is not protected under the First Amendment) might very well affect pornography in general, and *Hustler* magazine.

". . . I would like to state at the outset that I am opposed to child abuse or the exploitation of children in any manner," he said to the House Subcommittee. "[But] it . . . horrifies me . . . [that] . . . the first amendment [is] getting dragged into another murky situation. And I see this happening. I feel that somehow we must deal with child abuse and sexual exploitation of children through child abuse laws and not involve the First Amendment."

He added that he thinks education about sex is part of the real answer to combating child porn.

*From a professional point of view, pornography is my business, and I have over ten million readers of my magazine, [with] a combined readership, over fifty million. The majority of the letters that come into my magazine are from people that would like to see photographs of shaved genitalia. What they are really asking for is photographs of children, but they can't come out and say it.*

*There are millions of these dirty little old men out there, and legislation is not going to help it, it is going to make it worse.*

*I think we must direct our energies to a better understanding of why these problems happen in society.*[10]

Until 1984, only twenty states had strict antichild porn laws on their books. The federal government and the other thirty states had weak, practically unenforceable laws. These laws required that the prosecution prove that the offenders were producing obscene material. As we have already seen, because *obscenity* is difficult to define, it was next to impossible to get a conviction.[11]

But on May 21, 1984, President Reagan signed into law the Child Protection Act, which was created to clamp down on child porn. This new statute increased the penalties on child porn producers tenfold and granted new powers to law enforcement officials for wire tapes and seizures of pictures, equipment, and money in the possession of the people involved in the child porn operation. All that prosecutors had to do to close down the operation and prosecute the offenders was to prove that underage (younger than eighteen-years-old) children were involved.

Unfortunately, the new law has not wiped out the proliferation of child pornography in America, but it has made it easier to prosecute offenders.

The best weapon society has in fighting child porn or any other type of pornography is the pocketbook. Most likely, if people refused to buy child porn, it would not be able to survive. The reason it exists is to fill the pockets of its producers, distributors, and sellers.

In the next chapter, we will take a look at the *business* of pornography. Who is making the money? We will look at sales figures and profits. And, we will see why pornographers fight so hard to keep their money-making operations going in the face of mounting vocal opposition.

# THE BUSINESS OF
# PORNOGRAPHY

Of all the issues concerning pornography, business is the
key element. For without money, without profit, there
would be nothing to debate. While, of course, it is true
that if there were no willing buyers, there would be no
willing sellers, it is also true that the producers, distributors, and sellers of porn make large profits.

The dollars involved are staggering. Consider the following statistics reported in the *Ladies' Home Journal*,
October 1985:

- Americans spend $8 to $10 *billion* every year on
  sexually explicit material, more than the $6.2 bil-
  lion grossed by ABC, CBS, and NBC *combined*.

- More than 165,000 people are involved in the pornography industry.
- Sexually oriented magazines are bought by 20 million people every month.
- Ten to 15 percent of the videocassettes rented and sold in this country are sexually explicit films.
- Pornographic films can be produced for as little as $20,000–$125,000. They can then be sold, making a profit of up to $2 million in retail sales.
- Dial-a-porn lines receive hundreds of thousands of calls *daily* benefiting the phone companies.[1]

One reason that pornography is such a huge business is that porn has found a larger audience. Not long ago, most Americans were not exposed to sexually oriented reading material and never saw more than a passionate kiss on the movie screen. Pornography was limited to X-rated movies and "adult book stores" that sold magazines and sexual devices. These businesses were usually located in a "sleazy" part of town. "Men's magazines," catering to predominantly male audiences, were kept behind the counters of book and magazine stores and brought out only at the special request of acceptable-age adults.

All this has changed. Today, moviegoers can see nudity and love-making onscreen, both in movies and on cable television. With the popularity of videocassette recorders, people can buy or rent pornographic tapes to take home for private viewing. There are even sex computer businesses that provide subscribers with the network to send sexually explicit messages to other members.

One of the businesses to emerge from society's openness toward sex is "dial-a-porn." With one type, the caller receives a recorded message. With another, the caller contacts the business and makes arrangements to pay the fee (usually $35 for a half hour) using a credit card. The dialer is then called back by a woman who will participate in any type of sexual conversation the caller desires. These businesses have been very successful.

The telephone company also reaps huge profits as a result of dial-a-porn. The Final Report of the United States Attorney General's Commission on Pornography (which we will examine closely in a later chapter) reported that,

> *Dial-a-porn providers and the telephone companies realize significant revenues from the Dial-a-porn services. When a caller is charged on his monthly telephone bill for pre-recorded Dial-a-porn messages, the provider of the message and telephone (company) divide the revenues according to local tariffs. . . . At two cents per call in New York City, one major Dial-a-porn provider earned $16 thousand a day and a total of $3.6 million for the year ending February 28, 1984. The telephone company [which serves] the state of New York has earned as much as $35 thousand a day from Dial-a-porn calls.*[2]

Dial-a-porn got its start in 1982 when a well-known porn magazine, *High Society*, offered a new service: its monthly centerfold model recorded an erotic message on an answering machine. The response was so enormous that the company, which started out with twenty answering machines, added eighty more, and soon acquired one of New York Telephone's mass announcement lines.[3]

Dial-a-porn lines range from bestiality to child sex and rape. The phone numbers are advertised in porn magazines, so anyone who can obtain one of the magazines has access to the Dial-a-porn lines.

Many people are concerned about the large numbers of under-age callers. There have been several instances, reported heavily in the media, of parents receiving $200 telephone bills, only to discover that their children have been making long distance calls to Dial-a-porn companies.

An article in the July 1987 issue of the *Journal* published by the National Federation for Decency, quoted U.S. Attorney, Brent Ward, as stating that of the 2.8 million callers who patronized the Dial-a-porn operations he prosecuted, "many, if not most, were ages 10–16." (A new statute passed by Congress in 1983 makes it unlawful for Dial-a-porn companies to distribute obscene messages by phone to minors or to anyone who does not request them.)

However, minors are not the only people calling the dial-a-porn lines. Recently, an audit of the Defense Department revealed that employees were making regular long-distance calls from the Pentagon that amounted to $25,000 *monthly*. (Who paid the bill? The taxpayers.)[4]

Fred Bruning, a writer with *Newsday* in New York, wrote in the June 27, 1983 *Maclean's* magazine, "Heavy thinkers already are worrying that the popularity of dirty telephone talk must mean that we have become a terrifically lonely, sad and isolated bunch. Insecure and unhappy in our real-life relationships, we look for fantasy substitutes."

One of the most popular forms of "private porn" viewing is on home television sets. With the advent of cable television and videocassette players, Americans can view pornographic movies right in their own living rooms. A 1985 *Newsweek* poll indicated that 9 percent of those interviewed had either bought or rented an X-rated movie

*Thanks to the home-video market, the multi-billion dollar porn film industry is reaping record profits.*

—90

cassette during the past year. That figure is equal to almost 40 percent of all VCR owners, according to *Newsweek*. "When people buy their tape deck, they buy a kiddie movie for their child and an X-rated movie for themselves. It's the standard starter kit," says New York's Video Shack chain president, Arthur Morowitz.[5]

The *Ladies' Home Journal*, in October 1985, reported that many experts believe that the growth of porn is directly related to the growth in new technology, rather than a growing desire of Americans to see porn. "Being able to see anything you want to see when you want to see it in your own home is very appealing," stated Dr. Clive Davis, a social psychologist at New York's Syracuse University. "Couples view it partly out of curiosity and partly to become aroused. When it doesn't offend or disgust them, they're apt to look at it again."

X-rated movie theaters still have a following. About 100 of these films are made every year and play in 700 X-rated theaters around the country. Two million Americans buy two million tickets every week, making the X-rated movie business a $500 million industry. And that figure does not count the money made when the films are sold in soft-core versions to cable television.[6]

An X-rated movie production company can usually count on doubling its investment. The budgets are smaller for porn movies than for other commercial films. *Newsweek* investigated one typical production and found that it was made on a $120,000 budget with a crew of eighteen people in just five long shooting days. "It takes that many people to get lunch at Paramount," remarked accountant-turned-producer Les Baker in the article.

Because of the low budget, *Newsweek* reported, there are no frills. True, there is a "star" system in the porn market (the female star of the film in the *Newsweek* article was earning $1,500 a day; the male star, just $750 a day), but as little as possible is spent in other areas. The number of locations are kept to a minimum so that the crew will not waste valuable time setting up their equipment. There are usually no rehearsals for actors and crew. *Newsweek* reported: "The low-rent approach applies to the cast, too: on the second day of the shoot an actor playing a body builder sacrificed his screen debut because he had received a better offer to paint a house. A replacement was hired over the telephone. 'We're flexible,' says Baker. 'This isn't Shakespeare.' "[7]

Adult bookstores have also increased in number in recent years. In a February 24, 1981, article in *Family Circle* magazine, writers Linda Tschirhart Sanford and Mary Ellen Donovan report that there are more than 15,000 of these stores in the United States. "That's three times the number of McDonald's restaurants, boasts *The Adult Business Report*, trade newsletter of the pornography industry."

Furthermore, the article says, the number of pornographic magazines has also increased to more than 400, read regularly by up to twenty million men and boys, according to one estimate.

Antiporn activists have had some success in recent years in their fight against "adult" bookstores and other outlets that sell pornography. These successes have been, in large part, the result of boycotts and picket lines in front of these establishments.

For instance, there are no longer any bookstores catering to porn lovers in Atlanta, Georgia. *Hustler*, a well-known "skin" magazine, is not available anywhere in the city. Similar results occurred in Cincinnati, where porn is not sold. Virginia Beach, Virginia, and Williamson County, Texas, have both been targets of victorious antiporn crusaders. The Playboy channel was dropped from cable television in some cities as a result of citizens demanding that it be taken off the air. And 2,000 volunteers in Fort Wayne, Indiana, spent two years picketing porn businesses. Finally, a new prosecutor was elected and all pornographic businesses were closed.

Even though antiporn activists have had some success in scattered areas in reducing the amount of porn available to the public, it is most unlikely that they will succeed in eliminating the pornography business. The large profits available to producers and marketers provide strong incentives to keep their operations flourishing.

*In some places, such as Cincinnati, pornography is gradually disappearing.*

—95

# THE
# AMBIVALENCE
# OF AMERICANS

Americans believe in, and strongly support, their right to buy, read, or print what they like without government intrusion. On the other hand, they are alarmed at the proliferation of pornography—particularly porn using violence and exploiting children.

American social values tend to swing back and forth like a pendulum from the right (with more traditional, conservative values) to the left (which has a more open, permissive view of individual freedom).

In the past sixty years in the United States, society has swung from conservative to liberal several times. During the Roaring Twenties, the time of the "flapper" and speakeasy (a place where liquor was sold illegally during Prohibition), the pendulum had swung to the liberal side. But by the 1930s, during the Depression, American values had swung conservative and traditional family ties became of the utmost importance again. The 1950s was still a relatively innocent time, but by the 1960s and 1970s, the pendulum had swung back to the left.

But now, in the 1980s, many Americans have shown by their votes that they have made the swing back to the right. Traditional family values are back in vogue, and along with it, a desire for religious and moral leadership. President Reagan won his office in part by appealing to society's desire to reclaim a more conservative social outlook. But a conservative society also values the rights provided for in the Constitution, including the right to speak and write *without government involvement.*

These philosophies might seem contradictory. How can people who believe that pornography must be stopped also believe that the government should not interfere with what we print or speak? This, then, is the *ambivalence* of Americans concerning pornography. (Ambivalence means the existence of conflicting emotions at the same time.)

People who support the First Amendment argument for allowing pornography to exist believe that there are many dangers inherent in restricting what we are allowed to read or say. If the government begins setting rules for what kinds of reading materials are "appropriate" in this country, they say, what other kinds of reading matter might be outlawed simply because those in the government don't like what they say? Who would judge which books, articles, newspapers, movies, or short stories would be allowed to exist? And on what grounds would these people be able to censor the media? Many Americans believe that allowing censorship of any kind opens the door to the abuse of our constitutional rights.

*The two sides of porn*

The July 21, 1986, issue of *Time* observed, "While polls show that many Americans have a renewed appreciation for traditional values, their toleration of their neighbor's right to reject those values has not declined at all. Notes California pollster Gary Lawrence: 'More people than ever are embracing moral traditional values. But they're saying they don't want anything to be repressed or oppressed, either.' "

*Newsweek* published the results of an early 1985 Gallup poll in their March 18, 1985, issue. It reported that almost two-thirds of those interviewed supported a ban on magazines, movies, and videocassettes that feature sexual violence. Also, about three-quarters of the people surveyed agreed with antiporn feminists that sexually explicit material "leads some people to lose respect for women and leads some people to sexual violence."

On the other hand, "clear majorities favored the continued sale of X-rated movies and sexually explicit magazines, although some were willing to limit public display." (Remember, as we learned in an earlier chapter, almost 40 percent of all VCR owners interviewed indicated that they had either bought or rented an X-rated movie during the past year.)[1]

*Newsweek* used another example to illustrate America's mixed feelings. Society has collectively cried out in horror about scandals involving the sexual abuse of women and children. But that same society spends $5 billion each year supporting in the marketplace a business that promotes and teaches men and boys about the sexual exploitation of women and children.

Americans do have ambivalent feelings about pornography, and many can argue passionately on both sides of the issue.

As Gunnar Myrdal, the Swedish Nobel laureate, once pointed out, "Americans will say, practically in the same breath, 'No one can tell me what to do' and 'There ought to be a law against that.' "[2]

The pendulum swing to the right was in evidence in the summer of 1986 when the Meese Commission on Pornography made its report public after a one-year study of the subject. In the next chapter, we will look at what conclusions the Commission reached and how the public responded.

# THE MEESE
# COMMISSION ON
# PORNOGRAPHY

In the summer of 1986, a final report was issued by Attorney General Edwin Meese's Commission on Pornography. The release of the Commission's report was a highly publicized media event, and its findings were radically different from a 1970 report of the President's Commission on Obscenity and Pornography.

The 1986 report, a two-volume, 1,960-page document, was the result of a year-long, $500,000 government-sponsored investigation. The Commission's job, according to Meese, was to study pornography's impact on society and to recommend "more effective ways in which the spread of pornography could be contained." Unlike the 1970 Commission (which had a $2 million operating budget, a twenty-two-member staff, and two years to complete its study), the Meese Commission sponsored no original research. Its advisers were mostly policemen and antiporn activists. Of the eleven panel members, six were well-known supporters of government-sponsored antiporn measures against sexy books and films. According to the *New Republic*, "The Meese commission lacked the financial and staff resources of its predecessor, but since its conclusions were preordained, it didn't really need them."[1]

The report was released at a Justice Department news conference during which Edwin Meese accepted the document from Chairman Henry Hudson. Reporters at the scene took particular delight in pointing out to their audiences a detail that the news conference organizers surely failed to notice: Mr. Meese accepted the report standing in front of a semi-naked statue of a female figure representing the "Spirit of Justice."

The most important conclusion in the Commission's report was a link between violent pornography and aggressive behavior toward women. This conclusion was based on the fact that in recent years, as porn became increasingly more violent and sexually graphic, the incidence of violent sex crimes increased. There was no proof offered that one was the *cause* of the other, but the facts were cited by Commission members and the assumptions about a causal relationship were made.

The Commission also stated that exposure to nonviolent sexually explicit material that degrades women also has "some causal relationship to the level of sexual violence."

The Commission's conclusions directly contradicted a report issued by President Nixon's Commission on Obscenity and Pornography, which, after careful study and research, refused to draw any cause-and-effect conclusions.

The Meese Commission report brought up a finding that Edward Donnerstein, at the University of Wisconsin,

had suggested in his 1984 studies: that sexually violent pornography "leads to a greater acceptance of the 'rape myth,' " (that women want to be forced into sex, physically hurt by it, and raped.) The Commission also pointed out another fact that Donnerstein had already reported: that nonviolent pornography which can be described as degrading to women contributes to a lessening of concern in males toward rape, but does not necessarily promote violence.

The Commission reported that there was no evidence that nonviolent, nondegrading erotica causes violence, but they refused to label it as harmless.

The Meese Commission did not expand on the legal definition of obscenity, but accepted the Supreme Court's guidelines, which, as we have seen, are based in part on local "community standards."

But the Commission did recommend that federal laws be passed to facilitate the seizure of porn assets from the industry's producers, and that unfair labor practice laws be written to make it easier to prosecute producers who hire porn performers.

The Commission further suggested that the Federal Communications Commission (FCC) curb porn programming on cable TV and "Dial-a-Porn" telephone operations. In addition, the Commission suggested that peepshow booths in porn shops should not be built with doors, hoping that the lack of privacy might curtail sexual activity inside.

The Commission, particularly concerned with child pornography, recommended that laws be passed which

*Attorney General Edwin Meese's report on porn called for sweeping changes in federal and state laws to eradicate pornography.*

would make the knowing possession of child porn a *felony*. (A felony is a crime which is more serious than a misdemeanor.)

In February 1986, five months before the release of the report, Alan Sears, a federal prosecutor and executive director of the Commission, wrote to several large companies informing them that the Meese Commission had "received testimony alleging that your company is involved in the sale or distribution of pornography." He added that the Commission's final report would include a list of "identified distributors" of porn. Sears asked them to respond, adding a warning that failure to respond "will necessarily be accepted as an indication of no objection."

The letter that Sears sent to Southland Corporation (the company that owns 7-Eleven stores) included a photocopy of a page that said, "The general public usually associates pornography with sleazy porno bookstores and theatres. However, many of the major players in the game of pornography are well-known household names. Few people realize that 7-Eleven convenience stores are the leading retailers of porn magazines in America." (The author of the photocopied material was not named in the letter, but was later identified to be the Reverend Donald Wildmon, executive director of the National Federation for Decency. His statements about 7-Eleven stores were taken from his testimony before the Commission.)

Several weeks later, Southland yanked *Playboy* and *Penthouse* from its stores. *New Republic* writer, Hendrik Hertzberg, commented in the July 14 and 21, 1986, issues: "Their removal from their largest sales outlet by what amounts to government intimidation does not improve the political health of the country."

*Playboy* and *Penthouse*, along with the Magazine Publishers Association, filed suit. The federal district court ruled against the Meese Commission and gave the Justice Department five days to write all the companies it had contacted. The Justice Department was ordered to explain to the companies that their original letter did not mean to imply that their publications were obscene or to threaten to blacklist them. The federal court also prohibited the Commission from publishing the Reverend Wildmon's letter.

The section of the Meese Commission report that was probably the most widely publicized and commented upon was the thirty-seven-page-long list of suggestions on how citizens might combat pornography. These recommendations might sound familiar because they are very similar to those suggested by such groups as the National Federation for Decency and religious writers in *Christianity Today*. For instance, one suggestion details how people might form committees whose purpose it would be to write letters to prosecutors, judges, or police officials to inform them of their opinion of individual cases—how they were investigated and brought to trial. Another suggestion informs citizens what to expect when they monitor rock and roll lyrics: "Many popular idols of the young commonly sing about rape, masturbation, incest, drug usage, bondage, violence, homosexuality and intercourse."[2]

It is interesting that the Commission voiced moral judgments about society in the 1980s. "We all agree that some degree of individual choice is necessary in any free society, and we all agree that a society with no shared values, including moral values, is no society at all. . . . Although there are many members of this society who can and have made affirmative cases for uncommitted sexuality, none of us believes it to be a good thing."[3]

The report, which was available to the public for $35, was widely reported as containing a 300-page run of quotes taken directly from such movies as *Deep Throat*, *Debbie Does Dallas*, and *Biker Slave Girls*; from such sexually explicit books and magazines as *69 Lesbians Munching* and *The Tying Up of Rebecca*. These quotes consisted of dialogue and the kind of sexually explicit descriptions the commission sought to condemn. (Carole S. Vance, in the

*Nation*, wrote that the report's 1,960 pages "faithfully" reflected "the censors' fascination with the thing they love to hate.") It also contained descriptions of photographs from such magazines as *Tri-Sexual Lust* and a list of 2,370 film and 725 book titles that contained sexually explicit material.

The Meese Commission members heard from 208 witnesses, including 68 police officials and members of vice squads, 30 self-described "victims" of pornography, and 14 people representing various antiporn groups. They traveled to Chicago, Houston, Los Angeles, Miami, and New York and visited such places as Mr. Peepers, a porn shop in Houston.

Carole S. Vance, reporting in the *Nation* in the August 2/9, 1986, issue, said

> *Witnesses appearing before the commission were treated in a highly uneven manner. Commissioners accepted virtually any claim made by antipornography witnesses as true, asking few probing questions and making only the most cursory request for evidence or attempts to determine witness credibility. Those who did not support more restriction of sexually explicit speech were often met with rudeness and hostility, and their motives for testifying were impugned. The panelists asked social scientist Edward Donnerstein if pornographers had tried to influence his research findings or threatened his life. They asked actress Colleen Dewhurst, testifying for Actors' Equity about the dangers of censorship in the theater, if persons convicted of obscenity belonged to the union, and if the union was influenced by organized crime. They questioned her at length about the group's position on child pornography.*

The writing of the Commission's first draft of the report was supervised by former assistant U.S. Attorney Alan

Sears, the antipornography activist who was responsible for the letters that had been sent to the Southland Corporation and other companies. That report, relying heavily on the kind of sensational and bizarre testimony described above, was criticized by other members of the Committee as being overzealous. One Committee member, Frederick Schauer, a University of Michigan law professor, "to avoid having it become a laughingstock," wrote a 200-page draft that became the core for the final draft. This version took greater care to consider the rights of free speech and privacy. (The original draft had included a section on constitutional law which Schauer said was "so one-sided and oversimplified that I cannot imagine signing anything that looks remotely like this." About the testimony from porn "victims," he wrote, "If this section is included as is, we will have confirmed all the worst fears about the information on which we relied, and all of the worst fears about our biases.")

The July 14 and 21, 1986 issues of the *New Republic* say of Shauer's draft, "Though the draft has its share of howlers, on the whole it is reasonable and civilized in tone. It is written in a calm, even stately style. It contains little in the way of hysteria. To the limited extent that it takes note of the views of those who disagree, it treats those views with civility. Yet it preserves the basic conclusion Meese had programmed the commission to reach."

Two commission members, Judith Becker, director of the Sexual Behavior Clinic at the New York State Psychiatric Institute, and Ellen Levine, *Woman's Day* editor, were dissatisfied with the final report because it claimed that pornography causes sexual violence. They wrote an eighteen-page rebuttal in which they said that the panel's "efforts to tease the current data into proof of a causal link . . . simply cannot be accepted."

The weakness of the report was the lack of scientific studies that would have either proven or disproven the theories about the effects of pornography on the public.

(Social scientist Edward Donnerstein called the Meese Commission's conclusions "bizarre.")[4] They relied, instead, on the testimony of people involved in the porn industry, victims of porn, and police officials; already published studies; and "common sense." The result, then, was a report that drew conclusions based largely on anecdotes and unsubstantiated theories.

Because of the suggested link of violence and sexual *attitudes*, some people accepted the report's conclusions. Others, who were concerned about the proliferation of graphic pornography since the 1970 report, felt that the moral mood of the country justified the unproven conclusions.

Other people were critical of the report that focused on how *sex* harms society, rather than on how *violence* affects us.

The July 21, 1986, issue of *Time* reported the reaction of the University of Wisconsin psychologist, Edward Donnerstein, who studied porn and violence and refused to suggest a causal link to those who look only at the immorality of sex in the media, rather than looking at violence, including sexual violence. "Donnerstein is particularly perturbed by what he sees as the pervasive depiction of violence toward women on broadcast television and in movies. 'Why all the sudden talk about sex?' he says. 'Why do people find it offensive and violence acceptable?' " The emphasis, he suggests, should be on controlling violence.

The *Time* article went on to mention that TRB, a columnist in the *New Republic*, had pointed out that "while the Reagan Administration decries the spread of sexual pornography, the President has invited Sylvester Stallone, whose movies glamourize violence (and whose wife appears undraped in the current issue of *Playboy*), to the White House on more than one occasion."

The *Time* article also reported that American Civil Liberties Union lawyer, Barry Lynn, who attended Commission meetings in the six cities where testimony was heard, severely criticized the Commission's report, saying it was "little more than prudishness and moralizing masquerading behind social-science jargon." He said that the Commission members had already made up their minds about where they stood on porn long before they were appointed to the Commission committee. He pointed out that six of the eleven members had been crusaders for antipornography causes. "They truly want to regulate everyone's sex life," Lynn says in the *Time* article. "If they had their way, they'd like to crawl into your bedroom and tell you what is and is not appropriate."

Commission members were defensive about the ACLU's attack of the report, pointing out that they did not advocate censorship. Sociologist Park Dietz, a Commission panelist, pointed out in the *Time* article: "The big news here is that . . . the report says exactly the opposite of what the ACLU claims. It says that 'slasher' films are bad, *Playboy* is okay, and no books should be prosecuted."

But Lynn, answering Dietz's comment, said, "He can say that this is not about censorship. In fact, whenever you use the powers of the state or federal government to punish, to criminalize, to imprison people who sell certain kinds of sexually explicit material, that is censorship."

Some people argued that the thirty-seven pages of suggestions for citizen action against people who are involved in porn amounts to censorship. Legal scholar Geoffrey Stone from the University of Chicago says in *Time*, "To the extent the report directs private citizens to protest against constitutionally protected acts, there are serious First Amendment problems. The government has no business encouraging people to do things that it can't do."

Antipornography feminists hailed the Meese Commission report as being what women want. Catharine MacKinnon and Andrea Dworkin, who drafted the Minneapolis Antipornography Ordinance, commented that

the Commission "has recommended to Congress the civil rights legislation women have sought." Dorchen Leidholdt, founder of Women Against Pornography, said, "I'm not embarrassed at being in agreement with Ed Meese." She agreed with Commission members who wanted to publish Donald Wildmon's list of businesses that sell pornography.[5]

Carole S. Vance, in *The Nation*, commented that anti-porn feminists such as Dworkin and MacKinnon and the Commission had used each other. "The Meese commission used feminist language to justify its conservative agenda, while antipornography feminist groups used the Meese commission to gain public recognition and legitimacy."

The Meese Commission report probably did little to change anyone's mind about pornography. Those who had always been against the proliferation of pornography continued to fight; those making money in the porn business, and those who enjoy sexually explicit material continued to stand with those who feared the implications of censorship and the trampling of constitutional rights.

Even though the report (by the admission of the Commission's members) was unscientific and based largely on anecdotes, the conclusions reflected the moral mood of the country in the mid-1980s. The report was a product of the committee, when the pendulum had swung far to the right. It remains to be seen how the report will be judged by future generations.

*Barry W. Lynn, legislative counsel for the ACLU. The organization blasted the Meese commission for launching a "national crusade against dirty pictures" that missed the boat.*

# CONCLUSIONS

At the heart of the pornography issue are questions about morality, sexuality, and our rights as free men and women.

Many people look at only one side of the issue. Some individuals might declare pornography to be immoral and think that it should not exist because of its harmful effects on its readers or viewers. Others might only consider the negative effects on one group of people, women in particular. They point to the increasing incidence of violence against women and declare that any kind of pornography should not be tolerated. Still others think that the rights of a free press and free speech are the only worthy considerations. These people fight for the right of any printed material to exist, regardless of its content, because the

United States Constitution guarantees the right of a free press without government intrusion.

But, as we have seen, the pornography issue is not that simple. There is not just one side to consider. And at the heart of the dilemma is the very important question, what *is* pornography? When this general word is used to describe everything from sexual scenes in an R-rated movie to photographs depicting violent sexual encounters, there is bound to be disagreement on how we define the term and how we react to its availability.

We could replace the word "pornography" with "obscenity," which is the legal term, but when the courts apply community standards to their definition, one town's obscenity might be perfectly legal in another community.

Justice Potter Stewart once said that, though it was difficult to define, he knew pornography when he saw it. He was saying he knew what porn was to *him*. But one person's pornography could be another's art or literature. One person's standards cannot be used to determine what is obscene. That is why the courts in recent years have used, in part, "community standards" to determine whether a piece of material is obscene, and, therefore, illegal.

"Erotica," the term generally used to describe non-graphic, but sexually arousing material, is accepted by many people as harmless. But other people, and not only antiporn feminists and conservative church leaders, find pornography distasteful because they say it teaches men, using erotic images, that women are no more than the sum of their sexual organs. They point out that pornography portrays sex as having nothing to do with human feelings. "Anyman" is aroused by "Anywoman" and has a sexual encounter with her, whereupon he goes off in search of other prey. They describe pornography as basically antiwomen because porn presents a female figure who is not on the same level with the (presumably) male reader or male figure in the erotic image. She is there simply to please or arouse or satisfy him. (This view of porn does not take into consideration the fact that some porn is intended for, and used by, women.)

Many people (including those in favor of porn) accept these points as being true. Yes, they agree that pornography separates sex from feelings and, in many cases, reduces women to nothing more than sexual playthings for men. But, they say, are those reasons enough to *outlaw* porn? "After all, don't we have a right to read or view whatever we want? Isn't this a free country?" they ask.

So we are back to looking at the rights provided for in the First Amendment to the United States Constitution. However, if you remember, like some other forms of communication (such as yelling "Fire!" in a crowded theater or publishing lies about another person), the Supreme Court has determined that obscenity is not protected by the First Amendment.

And that brings us around again to the question, just what is obscene, and, therefore, illegal?

One part of the definition problem is that sometimes it is difficult to separate the sex from the violence. If we accept what we call "erotica," how much does the woman in the photographic image have to be dominated by the male for us to consider it an "abuser-victim" scenario?

Many people are alarmed about violent pornography. We have examined studies which indicate that sexually violent films affect viewer attitudes about women and cause viewers to trivialize violence against women.

There are even larger numbers of people who are alarmed about the use of children in pornography. Anyone who describes porn as a "victimless crime" is not looking at child porn. From young people just under the age of consent to babies under one year, children have been used and abused by pornographers.

An important point here may be the issues of *consent* and *safety* of the models used in pornographic material.

Most people, even some in the porn business, agree that nonconsenting adults, under-age models, and situations depicting violent sexual encounters have no place in the pornography business.

Pornography *business*. That's the key word in this issue. For without the business, without the profits, there would probably be no pornography. Porn exists because there are enough people—our neighbors, relatives, friends, and acquaintances—who pay money to buy it. If people stopped buying porn, the pornographers would most likely go out of business.

*Penthouse* publisher Robert Guccione said it himself in a series of ads that ran in newspapers around the country: "Just as I have every constitutional right to publish *Penthouse*, so you, too, have every right to read it or ignore it." So, too, do people have the right to react to porn in their locality.

Citizens have the right, if they choose, to read or view pornographic material—or to organize boycotts against it. As we have seen, groups of citizens against pornography have picketed businesses and organized boycotts that have effectively eliminated certain magazines from convenience stores and closed porn shops in their cities.

It is important that informed citizens consider all the questions involved in the porn issue, whether those questions be legal, religious, or moral. We might well ask ourselves who is benefiting from the existence of porn and who is being victimized? Then we can come to a decision about how the problems of pornography should be addressed in (as an article in *Newsweek*, March 18, 1985, put it) "a nation that sometimes seems to have lost its shame."

# SOURCE NOTES

CHAPTER ONE

1. Daniel S. Moretti, *Obscenity and Pornography: The Law under the First Amendment* (London, 1984), p. 1.
2. *Ibid.*, pp. 1–2.
3. *Ibid.*, pp. 2–3.
4. *Ibid.*, pp. 5–8.
5. *Ibid.*, pp. 18–19.
6. *Ibid.*, pp. 29–34.

CHAPTER TWO

1. Andrea Dworkin and Catharine MacKinnon, "Prohibiting Discrimination," *Pornography and Sexual Vio-*

*lence*, ed. Gary E. McCuen (Hudson, Wisconsin, 1985), p. 67.
2. *Ibid.*, p. 68.
3. Donald M. Fraser, "Protecting Free Speech," *Pornography and Sexual Violence*, ed. Gray E. McCuen (Hudson, Wisconsin, 1985), p. 71.
4. *Ibid.*, pp. 72–73.
5. "Porn Prone," *The Humanist* (July/August, 1985), p. 28.
6. "Pornography and Its Discontents," *Society* (July/August, 1987), p. 26.


CHAPTER THREE

1. Aric Press, Tessa Namuth, Susan Agrest, MacLean Gander, Gerald C. Lubenow, Michael Reese, David T. Friendly, Ann McDaniel, "The War Against Pornography," *Newsweek* (March 18, 1985), p. 60.
2. *Ibid.*, p. 66.
3. *Ladies' Home Journal*, (October, 1985), p. 162.
4. Richard Stengel, "Sex Busters," *Time* (July 21, 1986), p. 21.
5. *Ibid.*, p. 17.
6. *Ibid.*, p. 21.


CHAPTER SIX

1. Harry Genet, "Why People Don't Fight Porn," *Christianity Today*, (1982), p. 53.
2. "Innocence for Sale," *Ladies' Home Journal*, (April, 1983), p. 127.
3. *Ibid.*, p. 128.
4. Vicki Russell, "A Kiddie Porn Assault," *Macleans*, (June 7, 1982), p. 50.
5. Howard A. Davidson, "Child Sexual Exploitation." In Gary E. McCuen, *Pornography and Sexual Violence*, p. 78.

6. Vicki Russell, "A Kiddie Porn Assault," *Macleans*, (June 7, 1982), p. 50.
7. "Innocence for Sale," *Ladies' Home Journal*, (April, 1983) p. 128.
8. *Ibid.*, p. 130.
9. *Ibid.*, p. 127.
10. Larry Flynt, "Educate about Human Sexuality," as published in Gary E. McCuen, *Pornography and Sexual Violence*, pp. 84–87.
11. Phyllis Schlafly, "A Plan to Eliminate Child Pornography," as published in Gary E. McCuen, *Pornography and Sexual Violence*, p. 82.

## CHAPTER SEVEN

1. "The Pornography Explosion," *Ladies' Home Journal*, (October, 1985), p. 104.
2. "AT&T Dial-a-porn Rings Up Big Bucks," *Journal of the National Federation for Decency*, (July, 1987), p. 12.
3. *Ladies' Home Journal*, pp. 104–106.
4. *Journal of the National Federation for Decency*, p. 12.
5. Aric Press with Tessa Namuth, "The War against Pornography," *Newsweek*, (March 18, 1985).
6. *Ibid.*, p. 62.
7. *Ibid.*

## CHAPTER EIGHT

1. "The War Against Pornography," *Newsweek*, (March 18, 1985), p. 60.
2. Richard Stengel, "Sex Busters," *Time*, (July 21, 1986), p. 21.

## CHAPTER NINE

1. Hendrik Hertzberg, "Big Boobs," *New Republic*, (July 14 and 21, 1986), p. 21.

2. Richard Stengel, "Sex Busters," *Time*, (July 21, 1986), p. 14.
3. *Ibid.*
4. Carole S. Vance, "The Meese Commission on the Road," *The Nation*, (August 2/9, 1986), p. 80.
5. *Ibid.*

# FOR FURTHER
# READING

McCuen, Gary E. *Pornography and Sexual Violence.* Hudson, Wisconsin: Gary E. McCuen Publications, Inc., 1985.

Moretti, Daniel S. *Obscenity and Pornography: The Law under the First Amendment.* London: Oceana Publications, 1984.

Sheinfeld, Lois. "Banning Porn: The New Censorship." *Nation*, September 8, 1984.

Stengel, Richard. "Sex Busters." *Time*, July 21, 1986, pp. 12–22.

# INDEX

# ABOUT
# THE AUTHOR

*Carol Gorman is the author of five books, both fiction and nonfiction, for young adults. She is a language arts teacher and lives in Iowa with her husband and son.*